SO WHAT!
I'M STILL GOD'S GLAMOROUS GIRL

by DeeDee Freeman

Order this book online at www.trafford.com
or email orders@trafford.com

Most Trafford titles are also available at major online book retailers.

© Copyright 2010 DeeDee Freeman.

All rights reserved. No part of this publication may be reproduced, stored in a retrieval system, or transmitted, in any form or by any means, electronic, mechanical, photocopying, recording, or otherwise, without the written prior permission of the author.

Printed in the United States of America.

ISBN: 978-1-4269-3414-8 (sc)
ISBN: 978-1-4269-3415-5 (e)

Our mission is to efficiently provide the world's finest, most comprehensive book publishing service, enabling every author to experience success. To find out how to publish your book, your way, and have it available worldwide, visit us online at www.trafford.com

Trafford rev. 6/2/2010

 www.trafford.com

North America & international
toll-free: 1 888 232 4444 (USA & Canada)
phone: 250 383 6864 ♦ fax: 812 355 4082

DEDICATION

To my remarkable husband, Mike, I appreciate your love and desire to make me the happiest woman on the earth.

To my four beautiful children, Kevin & Brittney Borders (they have been married a year now…my how time flies), M. Joshua and Brelyn, I so admire the God in all of you. Stay committed to Jesus.

To my parents, James and Celestine Wooten (who just celebrated 60 years of marriage – when I grow up I am going to be just like them:) – thanks for demonstrating commitment to me. I love you both so much!

To all of the outstanding partners of Spirit of Faith Christian Center, I thank you for embracing me and allowing me to be a part of your lives.

Special thanks to Beetle Rice, and to my son, M. Joshua, for pursuing and cultivating the talent, that God has blessed him with, to design the book cover. I knew you could do it – I believe in you!

To all the ladies who wrote their testimony for this book, "THANK YOU" for sharing your unique stories with us. Don't forget, **So What, you are still God's Glamorous Girl!**

CONTENTS

Introduction		vii
Chapter 1.	Who Told You That?	1
Chapter 2.	So What!!	11
Chapter 3.	Divorcing My Emotions	17
Chapter 4.	What is a God's Glamorous Girl?	25
Chapter 5.	The Importance of VISION	31
Chapter 6.	Turning It Around	39

INTRODUCTION

I AM LEAPING with joy in my spirit while writing this book. I already know that thousands of women are going to be set free as a result of reading this message. This book is going to revolutionize your life. Those of you who need to be set free from past mistakes and decisions will be made free. Shackles will begin to fall off instantly. Satan's tactics will no longer be able to control you.

When God dropped in my spirit what I should write about, I began to pray and seek why. I wish I could say that it came to me right away, but it did not happen like that. It took me months to catch it, and I can really say, I got it." God said that this book would confirm ICorinthians 10:13:

> "No temptation has overtaken you except such as common to man, but God is faithful, who will not allow you to be tempted beyond what you are able, but with the temptation will also make the way of escape, that you may be able to bear it."

After reading this scripture, I thought about the counseling sessions I have had with women. The first thing most of them would say is that they feel like they are the only ones dealing with whatever they are dealing with. I would just smile, because I know the devil has no new tricks. This scripture in I Corinthians 10:13 will settle that:

> *"The temptations in your life are no different from what others experience. And God is faithful. He will not allow the temptation to be more than you can stand."*

The second thing most of the women would say is that they don't know why God is putting this on them, and then they would begin to talk about all the things they do right. Well, here again this same scripture says that God will not allow you to be tempted beyond what you are able. It never said He would put anything on you. Preachers have taught us that God won't put on you more than you can bear. "Oh, shut up and read your Bible," is what I want to say to those preachers. God said He won't allow, that means He must inspect the trial that's coming your way to make sure it's something you can handle. If not, He will not allow it into your life. Look at it this way, if it is in your life, you must be able to handle it. Sometimes we don't give ourselves enough credit. Then the third thing some would say is, "I don't know how to get over or out of this." Then here comes the last part to this scripture,

> *"When you are tempted, he will show you a way out so that you can endure."*

This was a "wow" moment for me, because God showed me that this book would show others that they are not alone, and that they are stronger than they think. This book will be a way of escape for many. I have gathered testimonies of successful women of God that have gone through some horrible situations but did not allow what they went through to control their lives forever. This book will help you to get rid of all the excuses of why you cannot make it. Regardless of your past defeats, you are still God's Glamorous Girl and So What!

CHAPTER 1
Who Told You That?

WHO TOLD you that you were not good enough, that you would never succeed at anything. Who told you that you were dumb, ugly, too fat, too short, too tall, too dark, or too white. Who told you that? Whoever told you that, did not have the right to give you a description of you. They were not responsible for creating such an awesome and unique person such as you. So, the only one that has the right to give you an identity is the creative God, our Father Himself. God gave definition to you long before you arrived here on planet earth. You are not just an outward expression of your parents' heated moment, but you were created in the express image of God the Father. Genesis 1:26 says,

> "Then God said, "Let us make human beings in our image, to be like us."

I wish someone would have told me this scripture when I was young. I was always too tall. I hated my height as a kid. The teachers would always form lines from shortest to tallest or put us in alphabetical order. Well, I was the tallest in class, and my last name was "Wooten", a double wammie. "Move to the back of the line," is something I would hear every day. You would not think that something like this could affect a child, but it did affect me. Feeling too tall, I would begin to stoop and slouch over to seem shorter, in order to fit in with my friends. I have a brother that's a year younger than me, and he must have my momma's genes, because he is much shorter than I. He would tease me and call me goofy names, and I would cry as if someone had beaten me. It was crazy.

Now, when I look back over my life, I see that this is where the struggle of low self-esteem began. I have four older sisters and two brothers. My mom never really taught us to be confident and to feel good about whom we were. I was never taught to speak up for myself. It took me years to learn that I had rights as a human, and that I did not have to take what everybody said or did to me. I will tell you more further in the book of how I transitioned. Going back to having four sisters, all of whom I adore and admire. They all were my role models growing up. I did not say they were all good role models, but they all were role models. Depending on the day, the moment, or how I felt, I would decide on which one I wanted to be like. My oldest sister received Jesus at a young age and got married. She was real saved: no pants, no make-up, long skirts kind of saved. She had her first child when I was eight years old, and I would catch the bus to go baby sit for her when she had to go somewhere. I thought, *this is the life, y*oung, married, nice husband, a baby and your own apartment. To me she had to be doing something everyone else was not doing. I had to find out what it was and I did. It was church. When she asked me to start going to church with her, I was so excited! We would go from sun up to sun down, dancing and singing praises to God all day. No, I really mean "all day long." Then I grew up and "all day long" church became a bit too much. So, I decided to pick another sister to follow. This sounds so funny to me. I picked another sister as if it was cotton or something. Well, I picked the sister that I was next to. Man, she was cool. She hung out all the time. She did whatever she wanted. She was my hero. No, I mean really, I idolized this girl. She wore the coolest boots and nicest jeans with a big afro bush. I remember when I was fourteen and had my first summer job, and I wanted a pair of frye boots like hers. So, she took me shopping and convinced me to get the ugliest thick rubber sole frye boots because she did not want me to have some just like hers. Because she told me they were cool, it settled me. Then as I got older I started to hang out with her some. This is when I first used marijuana, even tried cocaine. My life was in a spiral. I was going down quickly. I got away from that sister, because I realized that was not the life I wanted for me.

I just wanted to talk about those two sisters, so you could see the extremes of my life. I did learn from the other two as well. My mom was not a real strong influence in my life in the sense of being around her much. She worked and would come home and go to her room. I think she got tired when she had me. I was child number six. My second oldest sister really took care of me when I was a child. Being the youngest girl, I got everything I wanted from my parents and my siblings. DeeDee got what DeeDee wanted. Now, I know I haven't told you about my dad, so let's do that now.

Daddy, Daddy. I was and still am "Daddy's girl." I could do no wrong. If something went wrong, he knew it was not my fault. My youngest brother would hit me, and I would tell; and boy, did he regret that. We would fight every day. My dad would make him sit outside until he came home. "Don't mess with DeeDee!" My dad always made me feel real special. I started modeling, and he would come to my shows and take pictures that he would put on his wall at work. Out of seven children, I was the only one he bought a car. He bought a car for my three oldest siblings to share, but I got my own. I'm just painting a picture of the environment from which I came. You see, we all are the products of our environments, that's why it is important to raise our families in the word of God. I was being trained to be a "Wooten," but I needed to be trained to be a woman of God. Some of the things the "Wooten's" did, Christians wouldn't do.

I made a lot of poor choices and decisions based on how I felt. Most people would look at the security of my family structure and think that it should have been enough to help me. Well, it was not. I grew up empty, looking for someone to follow, to show me the way.

Thank God for college. That is where I met my girlfriend DeShawn. She was the first young real Christian girl I met that I wanted to be like. She never put pressure on me to live right. She just loved me and showed me how a Christian should be. I remembered being on a school trip, and I asked her to lead me to the Lord and she did. I thought my life would just change overnight, but it did not. I was waiting on God to change me or to fix me, and He did not. So, I struggled being a Christian, because my friend knew enough to get me saved but not enough to really help me. I needed someone to take me by the hand and show me. DeShawn did her part.

It is amazing how episodes in your life will expose who you really are. I got married at 21, thinking I was really ready to be some one's wife. Boy, how I had deceived myself. I was nowhere near being ready to be a wife. After all, I did not even know who I was. How could I bring something to the table, and I didn't know what I had to bring. I was a "hot mess"! I was spoiled, selfish, stubborn, and an emotional wreck. I had lied to myself for so long, telling myself that I had it together. I did great, as long as there were no challenges. Challenges became a part of my everyday life (ok, every other day). My husband and I bumped heads all the time. He wanted to be in charge, and so did I. After seven years of fighting, I gave in, or should I say caved in. I made some poor decisions and said a lot of nasty things that I wish I could take back. They were all based on how I felt about myself. I made decisions that would affect me and others negatively. I began to hate me. I sank so far to the bottom of the depression poll that it was crazy. I could not believe that my marriage was this bad. Nobody treats DeeDee this way. I am the baby girl that gets my way. I began to live in all the negative words that Mike, my husband, would call me. I told you earlier that I always followed one of my sisters, so I was good at following, but it had to be by choice and not force. After I had lost what little identity I thought I had, I figured I should find myself in his words. His words and my past put double pressure on me to just quit. Why fight to live? I would cry for hours, wishing I could just die. I had too much pride to tell anyone about what I was going through. So, I would pretend like everything was wonderful.

So many women can relate to what I went through with the verbal abuse. It is sad, but a lot of women live on the words of a man. Depending on what they say determines how we feel. If he says the right thing, we get up and are ready to produce the word, but don't let him say the wrong thing. The world shuts down. They act as if they are paralyzed. Please, I know, I lived it. I got to the place that I hated being this emotional wreck. Something had to be done, and the only thing that could fix my situation was the Word of God.

Praying for myself was interesting. I would talk to God telling Him all of what I was not. By the time I finished telling Him what I was not, at the end of my prayer I felt worse. All I did was rehearse what I believed about me. Then one day I heard the voice of God say to me, "Who told you that? I never said that to you." This was the beginning of a new day for me. I began to search the scriptures to find out who I was, so I could be who I needed to be to my husband, my children, and to me.

You know, it is not always that easy trying to convince yourself that you are not who you thought you were. Reading the scriptures sounded like I was reading about someone else. Come on; for example, Genesis 1:26 saying,

> "Then God said, "Let us make human beings in our image, to be like us."

That sounds like a joke. I know this lump of mess could not be created in His image. I was saying, "God, you are pretty messed up, if you are like me" (LOL). Then I kept searching, finding Psalms 139:14,

> "I will praise thee for I am fearfully and wonderfully made: marvelous are thy works; and that my soul knoweth right well."

and 1 Peter 2:9,

> "But ye are a chosen generation, a royal priesthood, a holy nation, a peculiar people that ye should show forth the praises of him who hath called you out of darkness into his marvelous light."

The more word that I would set myself to receive, the more convinced I was that this is who I really am. I started to live in the words of the one who created me. I am a God's Glamorous Girl, created in the very image of God. You know, even reading about Adam and Eve, they themselves were clueless to the fact of who they were. It was proven in Genesis 3:5 when the serpent told Eve the reason God did not want her to eat of the tree in the midst of the garden is because God knew that they would be like Him (God). Well, when He created them, He had crated them to be like Him. If they really knew that they were created in God's image, they would not have compromised so quickly. When you don't know who you are, you can be talked into almost anything.

So many Christians remind me of how my son Joshua

was. Here he is living in, driving in, dressing in, blinging in, and "everything else in" that he wants in life. My husband was always telling him that all this is yours. Joshua would say, "No thank you, because I want my own. I want to work for myself and move to Atlanta." Dude, wake up. Your daddy has already laid it out for you. Everything you could ever want or dream for is already yours. Why try and do your own thing. Well, I will tell you why. Because just like him, most Christians don't know who they are and what The Father has already laid out for them. Also like the prodigal's brother didn't know who he was. He got upset because his father put a robe and ring on his brother after he realized who he happened to be. Well, if the brother really understood that all of his daddy's stuff belonged to him too, he would not have tripped. Come on and say, "I know who I am."

Well, let's see, if you really know who you are? Who is this person you call you? Where did you get this identity that you have of yourself? Did you get this identity from the Word of God or did you get it from some human in the earth, who probably does not have a clue of who they are themselves? I have ministered to hundreds of women that lack definition of who they are. Some have never known, while others have lost their identity to the words of an abusive partner. It is always amazing to me when someone is asked who are they, and the first thing most begin to do is to tell what they do for a living. You are not your job, nor are you a bunch of negative words that some fool has called you. You are the blood brought, blood washed child of the Most High God. You are fearfully and wonderfully made. You are the handiwork of God. You are not a mistake. Even the angels have an understanding of who you are. Psalm 8:4 cries out,

> "What is man, that thou art mindful of him? And the son of man, that thou visit him."

It is a wonderful thing to know that I am on the mind of God. Listen, it is crucial that you stop living in the words of others and start living in the words of your heavenly Father. God the Father is the only one that has the right to give you your identity, since He is the one that created you. We give people too much power over our lives.

In one of my counsel sessions, I sat with this beautiful and strong woman. When she began to talk, I realized that what I was looking at was not at all what she was feeling. Let me explain. This tall, slim, beautiful, brown skin lady walks in my door, appearing to be strong, aggressive and confident. After talking to her in the first five minutes, I realized she was feeling: very unattractive, timid, passive, and had lost of all self worth. I found out that she had been a Christian for 15 years; very educated, nice career, making a nice living, had her own house and car, and was putting her daughter through college alone. Here I am impressed with what she has accomplished and the stability she had in her home when she was growing up. But, at the same time, I was confused as to why she was feeling and dealing with all these insecurities. Finally, after a long while, she gets to the point. "I have been in a relationship with a guy for five years and for the whole five years he has either verbally or physically abused me." She goes on to tell me the things he has called her: dumb, stupid, ugly, incompetent, and a lot of other stuff. She explained to me that when she met him, she was all those things I perceived her as being. But after being broken down by the man that once complimented her on all those things, she lost all of who she was. I began to tell her she did not lose who she is; she buried who she is. I would have never seen all of what I saw, if it had been lost. She has simply suppressed all of the great things about herself because she decided to take the identity given to her by a man she believe loved her. What a dangerous thing to succumb to, the words of someone who does not have the right to give you definition. I really feel for women who have been in several of these abusive relationships. They have yielded themselves to a lot.

I am so glad that God does not leave us there, if we want His help Psalm 46:1 confirms we can have it:

> *"God is our refuge and strength, a very present help in trouble".*

I like that, "Present help." I have heard deacons and preachers alike say, "Sometimes God will make you wait or suffer for a while." He is a "Present help in trouble." The question would be, "Are you in trouble?" All we have to do is call on the name of Jesus, and He will help us. Jesus said He was going away, but He was going to send the Holy Spirit to be our helper. Jesus did not leave us alone. He knew we would get into some situations, and we would need some help. Thank you, Jesus! I know I needed His help because I was a mess. I still need His help. It is a good thing when you can locate yourself. Some people are in total denial. You are the only one deceived. Only when you begin to be truthful with you about you, will you begin to get the help you need. What is wild is this: you do not have to be in an abusive relationship to encounter this poor identity. It could be anything you have felt like a failure in, for some people. For example, divorce- the devil will begin to tell you that you are a failure; you were not a good wife. You cannot do anything right. Man, he will roll the tape of every past failure or bad decision. If you are not convinced in the Word of God about who you are, you will fall for it. I have seen some of the most successful and strongest women fall in this trap. This is a warning to those of you who have not experienced this poor identity. Set your guards, do not allow the enemy to sneak in on you. Feed yourself the Word about who you are and whose you are. Do not become so confident in yourself that you do not constantly read your Bible to reinforce what God says about you. You are God's Glamorous Girl.

In order for you to really know who you are, you must develop a relationship with the Father. Because others have lied to you before, and you have allowed Satan to lie to you, and you have lied to you, it will be easy to think God will lie to you. However, Numbers 23:19 declares,

> "God is not a man, so he does not lie. He is not human, so he does not change his mind."

Baby, God will not lie to you. You are all of what He says about you. It is time you start to live in the words of a loving Father. He will not switch up on you and call you something different later. You cannot make Him mad enough. If you do not remember anything else I say in this book, remember this, John 3:16 shouts,

> "For God so loved the world, that He gave His only begotten Son, that whosoever believeth in Him should not perish, but shall have everlasting life."

God must have cared enough about you that He gave up His only boy. Awesome, you must be really special. You should make an agreement with yourself to never allow anyone to call you out of your name or out of the description that God has given you. Hosea 4:6 states,

> "My people are destroyed for lack of knowledge,"

There is a wealth of information in the Bible about who we are. The sooner you get in it, the better off you will be. God has called us to rule and win in life. The only way you and I can do this is to get a better view of who we are.

CHAPTER 2
So What!!

So what you have not been all of what you should have been. So what you have made many bad choices. So what you don't look like everyone else. So what you don't feel as beautiful or as smart as someone else. So what you don't dress like or make as much money as everybody else. You must learn that God does not define us by our past decisions or by how much or what we have. Man is the only one that does that. Man will hold you hostage to your past. God is not like man. I believe this is the phrase that everyone needs to learn to say, "So what!" Every time the devil reminds you of something you have done, you need to just say with a loud voice, "So what!" Stop crying over the poor choices and decisions you have made. It is done and in your past. You cannot go back and fix it. I understand that some are still dealing with the consequences of those choices. But you can choose today to stop allowing that bad decision to control where you are and where you are going.

As long as the devil can keep us locked into our past, he knows that we are not going to use our faith to believe God for better. He wants to paralyze you. Don't allow that sucker, that snake, that low life to keep you where you don't want to be. You have power over him. God has given us the power over our lives. You have to take the authority God has given you and change how you see you.

I know you feel bad about what you have done. I feel you. I have been there several times, but I got tired of beating myself up, and after I was finished with me, the devil would take his turn. The worst is when you are sitting in church and the preacher begins to preach about something you have done. You start telling yourself, "I know he is talking to me. I saw him looking right into my eyes. I know somebody told him what I did." (LOL) By the time the preacher finishes, between your own thoughts, the guilt, and the devils daggers, you are so beat up you cannot wait to get out of church, only to go somewhere to soak in more guilt. Here you go again on this emotional roller coaster. You have to be determined to get off of that ride and never return again.

So many Christians, especially women, are led by how they feel and not by what they believe. I know some have just read about making bad choices, and you are thinking this book is not for me. Oh no, it's for you, because I understand that some people are where they are emotionally because of the choices made by others. There are those that have been violated, and you had absolutely nothing to do with it. But here we go, "So What!"

You have to decide not to be a victim to some fool for the rest of your life. It was not your fault, and the devil will constantly make you feel like you are not worthy of anything because of what has happened to you. Hold your head high and know you are still God's Glamorous Girl. You are not the picture of what some person has created you to be. You are what God says you are and that settles that.

This is a fight I know, but guess what? God said, "We win". I Timothy 6:12 instructs us to,

> *"Fight the good fight of faith."*

It would not be a good fight if we did not win. God fixed the fight. He sent Jesus, our big brother, to kick the devils posterior and to knock his teeth out. Can you picture running from an animal that has no bite? I know, crazy isn't it; but people do it all the time. Even the scripture says in Isaiah 14:16, how we are going to look at Satan and gasp,

> "..is this the one who made the earth to tremble?"

God gave us a heads up on who this dude, the devil is, so we would not be afraid.

Most people do not have a real Bible description of who Satan is. We think he can take us out when he wants to. He cannot; if he could, we all would have been killed before we had an opportunity to receive Jesus. My dad was so funny before he really understood the scripture. He would say, "Don't mess with the devil, leave him alone." Listen! Set yourself to read the Bible every day. Be like the Bereans in Acts 17:11,

> "..they were more noble and open minded than the Thessalonians.."

Why? Because they received the word with all readiness of mind, AND they searched the scriptures daily to find out whether these things were so.

You will not be able to say "So What!, if you don't have confidence in this Word. You know, it is impossible to have confidence in someone that you do not know. The devil does what he does best. He feeds you with all the negative thoughts that you will allow him to. Then he will work on those around you that know about what you did or what you went through to put you down. If you do not know any Word you will faint. I read a scripture in the Message Bible that was awesome. When you find one that fits your situation, a light comes on. Write this down somewhere, so every time the devil comes to remind you of what happened, you can go to this scripture and get excited. Isaiah

40:1-2 cries out,

> *(1)" Comfort, oh comfort my people, says your God. (2)Speak softly and tenderly to Jerusalem, but also make it very clear. That she has served her sentence, that her sin is taken care of , forgiven! She has been punished enough and more than enough, and now it's over and done with."*

This scripture make me want to run around the room every time I read it. I cried like a baby the first time I read it. The guilt and condemnation of sin is horrific. The only thing that can set you free is the words of our Heavenly Father. Come on, stop, get ready, and say "So What!" Isaiah 40:1-2 says you have been punished enough. It is over. Now, you should know it was not God punishing you. We blame God for so much. Your choice punished you. People say all the time God is condemning me. The scripture in Romans 8:1 explains,

> *"There is therefore now no condemnation to those who are in Christ Jesus, who do not walk according to the flesh, but according to the Spirit."*

Condemnation only comes when we walk according to the flesh. Preachers for some reason teach the Holy Spirit will condemn you if you do something wrong. No, He will convict you to let you know you are about to or have done something wrong. God is a loving Father, He will not beat you over the head and constantly put you down. God gets no pleasure in reminding you of your past. He sees the end result, and He wants us to focus on the future and not the past. God see us in our future state. He is always calling those things that "Be not as though they were." The past will hinder you from moving forward. Shout, "So What!"

When God created you, He knew you would get off course and make some dumb decisions. Isaiah 46:10 reads,

"Declaring the end from the beginning."

God went to the end of your life and backed all the way up to the beginning and laid out everything that you would ever need to make it through life. There are no emergencies in heaven. God was totally prepared for you to be here on earth. So, everything you need to help you make it to your desired end is here in place. You just need to be sensitive to Holy Spirit so He can lead you there. Come on practice again and say, "So What!" You are really getting good at saying this. Come on, one more time, "So What!"

You need to surround yourself with some friends that truly love you and that you will allow to be honest with you. Good friends will help you stay focused. They will not allow you to soak in your misery. Something that amazes me is when people are going through, they withdraw from people. That is the worst thing you can do. You should never be left to you. We need each other.

James 5:16 (Amplified) confirms this:

> *"Confess to one another therefore your faults (your slips, your false steps, your offenses, your sins) and pray [also] for one another, that you may be healed and restored [to a spiritual tone of mind and heart]. The earnest (heartfelt, continued) prayer of a righteous man make tremendous power available [dynamic in its working]."*

I love this scripture. Every time people act like they can go at it alone, I show them this passage. We are not islands. God created us to be a part of one another. I know sometimes you want to be alone, and that is cool for a minute; but bounce back before you get too separated. We just have to make sure the friends we have around us are spiritual. How are they going to restore us to a spiritual state of mind in prayer if they are not spiritual themselves? Pray and ask God to send you a true friend, one that you can talk to and not be judged by them later. Sometimes people will act like they your friend, as long as you are of some benefit to them, but as soon as you need them, or they can not benefit from you any longer, they are finished with you. Ok, I know you have had some of those bad friendships, but do not allow those bad apples to spoil new relationships that God wants to bring into your life. We all need help with something. I know you think you got it all together. You probably got it together in some areas, but we need the supply of others. So, open up your heart and let someone in. "So What!, you have been hurt before. It is God's job to protect us. Psalm 119:165 states,

> *"Those who love your instructions have great peace and do not stumble."*

CHAPTER 3
Divorcing My Emotions

God's Glamorous Girls are girls that are emotionally strong, stable, and spirit led. They are not flakes, sometimes up and sometimes down. We as women have to get it together and keep it together. Our emotions can be an enemy to our faith. Whenever you are not in control of your emotions, you are not in control of your life. Sometimes emotions will make you feel like a nut, and sometimes they won't. Sometimes you feel happy, and sometimes you feel sad. Sometimes you want to stay married, and sometimes you don't. Sometimes you feel like others love you, and sometimes you feel all alone. Come on; I think you get what I am saying. Emotions can be dangerous. If you keep listening to them all the time, you will make some dumb and poor choices. It is imperative that you are in control of your emotions at all times. The Bible says in John 6:63,

> *"It is the Spirit who gives life, the flesh profits nothing."*

You see, when you operate in your flesh, it profits you nothing; and it will stop you from receiving God's best. If God tells you to do or say something at a particular time and you weigh it by how you are feeling, 9 times out of 10 you will not obey the voice of God. For one, God seemingly always goes against what we would commonly do in the natural.

Emotions will take you on this roller coaster and will not stop and let you off. The funning thing about it, is that a lot of people enjoy that ride. If they did not like the ride, they would not stay on it for so long. Our flesh wants to be pampered, and I am not talking about a pedicure and a body massage. No, it wants to feel sorry for itself sometimes. It will tell you, "You owe me this - Go ahead, sit here and cry; no one understands; you are the only one feeling this way." I know this is true. I lived this for a while, until one day I got tired of my emotions dictating to me how I was going to be from one day to the next. I started praying and asking God to take something away from me that He gave me. Guess what? He would not take them back. (LOL) So, I had to start searching and finding out what all these feelings were for and how could I deal with them. They were running me crazy. Just like some of you who are reading this book. You feel like you are at the end of your rope. You keep asking, "What am I going to do?" I am so happy you asked. You must first realize that your emotions are never going away. Listen! I did not say how you feel is never going away. When God created us, He did a marvelous job. He created us in His magnificent image. Emotions serve wonderful purposes. I am not a professional or have degrees in Psychiatry, but I do study the Bible. Our greatest example setter is Jesus Christ. Now it would not be fair to call Him our great example if He did not give or equip us with the same thing that He has on the inside of Him. How can you be my example in a fight or a game and you are on steroids and I in turn am on nothing. I will never measure up to your strength or have your end, if you have an advantage. You need to tell me you are on drugs or have some super human powers or something. Then I can go find someone that I can measure up to. This may come as a shocker to some, but Jesus came in the earth as a man, all man. He did not have any super natural powers. It would not have been fair to us. With all this being said, now we can look at our example. You know, the one we follow, Jesus the Christ.

Hebrew 4:15 exclaims,

> *"For we have not a high priest which cannot be touched with the feeling of our infirmities: but was in all points tempted like as we are, yet without sin".*

How could Jesus have been in touch with how we feel or what we go through, if He did not feel? Jesus felt and still feels our hurts and our pains. Do you know the story in Acts 7: 54,60 about Stephen being stoned to death. The Bible says Jesus stood up. Wait; if He did not feel anything why did He stand up. You have seen people hurting or going through something and you did not have any emotional ties with them, haven't you? I know without asking you that it did not bother you at all, okay, maybe a little. Why? Because it did not move you emotionally. Ok, now think about when someone that you care deeply for is hurting and the effect that it has on you. You stand because you have been touched by their pain and anguish. You are positioning yourself to help. What about this one? When Lazarus died in John 11:35, Jesus wept. The reason He cried is immaterial right now. What is paramount is the fact that He did cry. He used a set of emotions that the Father gave us. So now, what made Jesus a better example than most of His followers are demonstrating? Jesus never let His emotions control or rule over Him. Unlike most people....the devil will use our emotions to paralyze us to stop us in our tracks. Jesus never allowed that to happen to Him. Even when He was in the Garden of Gethsemane and He said, "If it be your will, let this cup pass from me." That would have been a breaking point for most people. To have suffered all that He went through and the rejection of men that He came to save, Jesus is a tough dude. It is written in Hebrews 12:2,

> *"Looking unto Jesus , the author and finisher of our faith, who for the joy that was set before Him endured the cross, despising the shame, and has sat down at the right hand of the throne of God".*

Jesus was able to channel all of what He went through to the end result. He saw you and I, and He knew we would need an example to follow. He knew His purpose in the earth and His faith in the Father. Jesus was not an emotional wreck, because He knew all of what He was experiencing was temporal. We trip and get all upset over events, people, and things that are not even worth what we are feeling. The Bible declares in II Corinthians 5:7,

> *"We walk by faith not by sight."*

We are not supposed to walk by our sense realm. We walk by believing that the word of God is true and that it shall come to pass. Galatians 3:11 confirms,

> *"..the just shall live by faith."*

This is not something we do based on how we feel. Regardless of how we feel, we must live, breathe, and have our being in faith. When you know the outcome of what you are believing God for, you will not allow yourself to trip in the process. No doubt, as soon as you decide to move forward in feeling better about who God created [you], the enemy is going to throw all kinds of negative emotions your way. Satan does not care about how you feel. Satan just does not want you to use your faith for anything. His beef or fight is against God, and he knows your faith is the key to pleasing God. Let's make the enemy mad and please God with our faith. Romans 6:22 decrees,

"But now being made free from sin, and become servants to God, ye have your fruit unto holiness, and the end everlasting life."

Now this passage says that we were made free from sin, not that God came to do away with sin. When you do research and look up *sin* here, it means our sin nature and our sin conscience. I wish God had done away with our sin nature or conscience, but He did not. But what He did do is put us in a position of authority over our decisions, so our sin nature or conscience could no longer dictate or control us. Who got the power? We got the power. (LOL)

This is where I got this "divorcing my emotions" from. It is just like an ex-spouse that has common property or children, and you have to deal with them about certain things or issues, but they no longer can control or dictate to you on how to handle things any more. They have a right to call or visit you, but you don't have to answer or open the door anymore. Just like these crazy emotions, they have a right to visit, because they are needed at times. We do have common property, which is this body; but when you come at me all crazy, tripping and carrying on, I do not have to let you in. As a matter of fact, I have a new man and His name is Holy Spirit. He is my leader and my guide. If you want to be a real Glam Girl, you must be led by the Spirit of God. God said that His true children are led by His Spirit. Ask yourself, "What is leading me?" If you cannot say you are totally led by the Spirit of God, you will be at the risk of being led by your emotions or by someone else's.

Being led by someone else is dangerous when you do not know who you are. There are folks waiting to lead others into the identity they want them to have. Just think, what if Jesus would have allowed others to identify Him as being less than what God had created Him to be. When folks saw Jesus and He was operating in so much wisdom, breaking the word of truth down, and they looked at Him and said, "That is Mary's boy, he's just a carpenter's kid."

He was, but not in the connotation in which they said it. They tried to play Him down as nothing, but you will never read in the scriptures about Him running home crying or depressed because of how others were treating Him. It is time that you know who you are, so you can walk in the same level of power and authority that Jesus did. On the next page, I have put a Divorce my Emotion paper. Fill it out, and every time you are about to trip, pull it out and look at it. Remind yourself you are no longer submitted to how you feel.

EXHIBIT A :
Certificate of Divorce My Emotions

EXHIBIT A

GOVERNMENT OF THE PEOPLE
DEPARTMENT OF HUMANSERVICES
CERTIFICATE OF DIVORCE
DISSOLUTION OF EMOTIONS AND FEELINGS

KINGDOM COURT ADMINISTRATOR: DR. DEEDEE FREEMAN		FILE NUMBER-JOHN 3:16
PARTIES TO BE DISMISED:	FIRST *EMOTIONS* MIDDLE *EMOTIONS* LAST *EMOTIONS*	
USUAL RESIDENCE OR ADDRESS: **SOUL**		CITY, TOWN OR LOCATION
COUNTRY	STATE	DATE OF BIRTH
PARTIES TO BE EMPOWERED: FIRST MIDDLE LAST		MAIDEN NAME
PERMANENT RESIDENCE-STREET ADDRESS **PRESENCE OF GOD**		CITY, TOWN OR LOCATION
DATES OF OFFENSE: *PAST*	CHILDREN TO THIS MARRIAGE: ABUSE, HATRED, BITTERNESS, REJECTION, LONLINESS, HURT, JEALOUSY, DEPRESSION, LOW SELF-ESTEEM	
ATTORNEY FOR PLAINTIFF: *JESUS CHRIST*	ADDRESS OF ATTORNEY **HEAVEN**	DATE OF DECISION **MAY ___, 2005**

THIS DECREE IS BASED UPON YOUR SALVATION AND WAS GRANTED OVER 2000 YEARS AGO. THE BLOOD OF JESUS HAS RATIFIED THE DATE ON WHICH THIS DECREE BECAME FINAL.

SIGNATURE OF CERTIFYING OFFICIAL **JEHOVAH GOD**	/	SIGNATURE OF EMPWERED PARTY

CHAPTER 4
What is a God's Glamorous Girl?

To better understand the definition of a God's Glamorous Girl, I looked up the word glamorous in the *American Heritage Dictionary and the Roget's II: The New Thesaurus, 3rd edition.*

<u>Glamorous</u> means: an air of compelling charm, allure, appeal, attraction, attractiveness, charisma, charm, draw, enchantment, enticement, fascination. The synonyms are basically the same words that the definition used but a few added: fetching, lovely, prepossessing, pretty, sweet, taking, tempting, winning, and winsome.

When I looked at how glamorous was described, I automatically thought of God Himself. He is all of these adjectives of the word glamorous. God wants us to be attracted to Him. So, He has the appeal that is enchanting, that will fascinate and entice you to want to serve Him. Listen. He is so attractive and alluring that His charisma is charming, sweet, and lovely which tempts you to want to be with and like Him. The man is prepossessing of my mind, always winning and winsome. Who would serve or even be attracted to a God that is opposite of all these words? Now, if He is all of this, and He created us to be in His image, then we should be all this. We should be using our power and influence to attract others to the Lordship of Jesus Christ. This is a God's Glamorous Girl.

When I first used this name for my conference I received so much back talk. Christians are the first to ridicule other Christians. I can handle it from whomever, but it would be much better if it was coming from the world. When Christians don't understand or agree with something, the first thing they do is attack, when they should try and research for understanding.

What do you hear when you hear God's Glamorous Girls? Do you hear pretty, cute, prim, proper, classy, beautiful, having it going on, sophisticated; or do you hear vain, stuck-up, thinking too highly of oneself, conceited, egotistic, narcissistic or bigheaded? One thing I have learned is that people will judge others based upon their own position in life. When a person has all her needs met, is helping others to get their needs met, is fulfilled in life, and is living the good life based upon the word of God, they would be considered a God's Glamorous Girl. On the other hand, when a person is not fulfilled in life, her needs have needs, she is living under the law and having some false sense of humility and doesn't have a clue of what the word says, that person could potentially be a God's Glamorous Girl hater.

It is amazing to me that we put the best in our homes, our cars, and even in our churches. Churches and homes today are some of the most glamorous architectural master pieces you would ever want to see. I'm talking about churches with marble, glass, brass, granite, plush seats, huge monitors, light shows and on and on. Homes are no longer the same either. When I grew up we had one bathroom for nine to eleven people, depending on who was living with us at the time. Incredible, why did we have extras living with us? We had the longest lines in the mornings. Praise God. Now, most homes have a bathroom in every room or at least on every floor. Why do you need all that? Answer-Because it is available. My whole point in going through all of this, is - we put the best in churches and in our homes not realizing that we are the church and home of the living God, and we expect God to settle for any kind of living space. Why reduce who God is, when He is used to living in the best. You need to read your Bible. God has streets made of gold and pearls for gates. In the book of Exodus, God told Moses exactly what He wanted His temple to be made out of. Why couldn't He use wood and bricks like everyone else? These materials (wood and brick) were available for Him to use, yet He chose to use the very best. He knew what quality He wanted to use to make the streets and the gates. God Himself used the very best, and He expects us to use the very best.

This is a long way of answering what a God's Glamorous Girls is, but I know by now you get my point. If God is giving us His best, why do we try to present any old thing to Him? Let me make this clear. God's Glamorous Girls have it going on in every area of their lives. They live holy and righteous lives presented to God in beauty. Exodus 28:2 it reads,

> *"And thou shall make holy garments for Aaron thy brother for glory and for beauty."*

God is so vain. (LOL) Why does the garment need to be beautiful? Just throw something on. It is amazing to me that God pays attention to detail - even the smallest details - I have found that paying attention to detail will take you straight to Excellence. I Chronicles 16:29 says,

> *"Give unto the Lord the glory due unto His name: bring an offering, and come before Him: worship the Lord in the beauty of holiness."*

Also, Job 40:10 confirms,

> *"Deck thyself now with majesty and excellency; and array thyself with glory and beauty."*

God told Job to deck his self out. God is so cool; back in the day we would say, "You are decked out." That meant you were cleaner than a Q-tip. Pastors that do not know the word have put so many people in bondage. They have taught ladies not to cut their hair, not to wear make-up, and not to wear pants. Read I Peter 3:2-9,

> *(2) While they behold your chaste conversation coupled with fear (3) Whose adorning let it not be that outward adorning of plaiting the hair, and of wearing of gold, or of putting on of apparel; (4) But let it be the hidden man of the heart, in that which is not corruptible, even the ornament of a meek and quiet spirit, which is in the sight of God of great price. (5) For after this manner in the old time the holy women also, who trusted in God, adorned themselves, being in subjection unto their own husbands: (6) Even as Sara obeyed Abraham, calling him lord: whose daughters ye are, as long as ye do well, and are not afraid with any amazement. (7) Likewise, ye husbands, dwell wit them according to knowledge, giving honor unto the wife, as unto the weaker vessel, and as being heirs together of the grace of life; that your prayers be not hindered. (8) Finally, be ye all of one mind having compassion one of another, love as brethren, be pitiful, be courteous: (9) Not rendering evil for evil, or railing for railing; but contrariwise blessing; knowing that ye are thereunto called, that ye should inherit a blessing."*

In verse two the word *conversation* can be exchanged for *lifestyle* and verse three and four does not say don't adorn yourself. It is saying fix it up, but win your husband over by your inward beauty. Men are attracted to beauty. They are stimulated by sight. So, every woman needs to fix herself up, inwardly and outwardly. You cannot have a nasty attitude and look good on the outside and think that this is ok. No, you must have it together inwardly and outwardly.

The problem comes in when we have this unrestrained indulgence in fixing ourselves up outwardly, but we expect people to just deal with us if we have a nasty attitude. I have heard people say, "This is just how I am, accept it, or you don't have to deal with it." Now, I am talking about believers here, so this type of response is totally unacceptable. Why? I am glad you asked. God says in His word that we have been created in His exact same image and likeness. So with that said, do you think that God has a nasty attitude? I don't think so! A God's Glamorous Girl is well balanced. She is beautiful on the outside and beautiful on the inside.

So again, it is ok to fix yourself up. Put on some makeup, paint that temple, comb your hair, fix your teeth, and put on clothes that are clean and representative of a Christian. I encourage you, I admonish you, I beseech you. I hope you get my point , Fix Yourself Up!!!! On the other hand, we do not have to look like the world either to consider ourselves as fixing it up: our backsides should not be out, our cleavage should not be out, and our stomachs should not be showing. I have learned that women who feel inadequate or insecure about themselves, will compromise their dress. Some women feel like the only way they can get attention is by showing off their bodies. There is much more to us women than our nice curves (LOL). You see, how I threw "me" in there too (_our_ nice curves). We do not have to compromise our standards to get attention. Would you want Jesus to be standing in front of you or behind you with all your flesh out? I'm just asking! No we are trophies in the hand of God being showed off to the world on how a real Christian lady looks. Let the spirit of God help you get dressed. If you have any questions about what you are about to put on, stop and do not put it on. I am not trying to put anybody in bondage, but come on, let's raise the standard. Let us be God's Glamorous Girls.

CHAPTER 5
The Importance of VISION

Habakkuk 2:2,3 states,

> *(2)"And the Lord answered me, and said, Write the vision, and make it plain upon tables, that he may run that readeth it. (3)For the vision is yet for an appointed time, but at the end it shall speak, and not lie: though it tarry, wait for it; because it will surely come, it will not tarry."*

THE SCRIPTURE is clear that we should write down what we see for ourselves. Put it before you all the time, so you can run for it. Go get it, and make it happen. It will not be that easy to get you off track, when some joker comes to you and tries to get you to compromise your standard or tear you down, when you have vision before you. You should recall where you see yourself in the next six months or a year, and then ask yourself the questions, if I do this, will it hinder or delay where I am going? If your answer is *yes*, you will run the other way. So many ladies and men fall, because they do not have vision for their lives. It is easy to get someone off course who does not know where she is going. Vision will give you restraint. It will hold you in place. I remember when I first got married and we moved in this condo. Without stress, we could pay with ease. We went everywhere and brought anything we wanted, until one day we decided it was time to move into a single family home. What a huge step that was going to be. We did not have a dime saved up. We spent as fast it came. We thought tomorrow was going to take care of itself! You talk about crazy and young. I thank God nothing ever went wrong that would have needed a large sum of money. We were young, foolish, and in love. I remember as soon as we made that decision, things began to change. Decisions we used to make, we didn't make anymore. We would wake up in the middle of the night and say, "Let's go to New York." We would jump up, and then it would hit us that we wanted a new house. We would just turn over and go right back to sleep. Why? Because we were working on something. You must start seeing yourself better, so you can start working on something. Proverbs 29:18 declares,

> "Where there is no vision, the people perish: but he that keepeth the law happy is he."

When you do not have a vision for your life, you will cease from existence. You will feel like nothing, when you do not see yourself as something. Stop just living inside of everybody else's dreams and visions. For some people, all they have done is to live out what others have dictated to them. God gave you a brain for a reason; use it. If you are in a bad relationship and single, see yourself out of the relationship and go. You see, I had to be real clear in saying if single and in a bad relationship. If not, no doubt some married person would have taken that at face value and ran with it. Now for the married, if you are in an abusive relationship, see yourself out of it and go. Believe God for better; it is your call. Stop just going through the motions. Take charge of your life and see yourself living out the plan of God for it.

Take a few moments and write down on the next page where you see yourself in the future. Get a plan and run with it. Vision will allow you to press through all the opposition. I remembered when my marriage was bad. I would see what I was believing God for and not what I was getting. This allowed me to operate in my faith and continue to have hope. Most people focus on the negative. That is why it is crucial to get a positive picture in view. What you concentrate on will have the dominate influence in your life. I choose to focus on what I want in Christ.

VISION

In the next six months I see myself

_____
_____
_____
_____
_____
_____
_____
_____
_____
_____
_____
_____
_____
_____
_____
_____

DeeDee Freeman

In the next year I see myself

So What! I'm Still God's Glamorous Girl

In five years I see myself

CHAPTER 6
Turning It Around

IN THIS chapter you will read some powerful testimonies of some awesome women of God. You will see that regardless of the choices you have made in life, it is not too late to turn things around. Isaiah 46:10 says,

"Declaring the end from the beginning."

God knew when he created you that you would make the choices that you have made. He also knew that some would violate others causing them to feel the way they do about themselves or life itself. So God knowing all went to the end of your life before you arrived here on earth and laid out everything that you would ever need to help you get back on track. One of the things He laid out to help you and others are these testimonies you are about to read. You may not have experienced the things that these ladies have gone through, but I guarantee you, if you take the principles they have applied to their lives and apply them to yours, you will see that you too can be the over comer that God has made you. The devil has strapped us long enough to our past. Now it is time to be what God has laid out for us to be. Remember Isaiah 40:1-2 (Message) exhorts,

(1) "Comfort, oh comfort my people, says your God. (2)Speak softly and tenderly to Jerusalem,

but also make it very clear. That she has served her sentence, that her sin is taken care of, forgiven! She has been punished enough and more than enough, and now it's over and done with."

Get a grip and move forward. So what, if I have royally messed up in the past, I am still God's Glamorous Girl.

Testimony #1

There are many incidents that have happened in my life that could have broken me, but by the grace of God, I am still standing strong. An abusive relationship led me to seek help and guidance from my pastors. Here is my story.

In April 2008, after an argument with my boyfriend of over three years, things got physical. He ripped my shirt and struck me in my head. I picked up the phone to call the police and he jumped on top of me fighting to get the phone out of my hand. I held on to the phone for dear life and was relieved when I heard, "Alexandria Police Department, what's your emergency?" The 911 operator stayed on the phone with me until the officers came out. Unfortunately, the response that I was hoping for wasn't what I received. He had struck me in my head leaving no visible signs of abuse, so all they could do that night was ask him to leave.

For the next couple of days, I sat home and cried thinking….after all these years of abuse, I finally get the courage to call the police and this is the response I get???? You see, I had endured years of abuse at the hands of this man, starting on my 30th birthday. He said I acted as though I didn't appreciate the gift he had given me. He threw me to the ground, got on top of me and began punching me in the chest. I was in shock, I should have left then, but didn't. Then there was another instance when he dislocated my thumb while trying to grab a phone out of my hand. Again, I should have left, but didn't. Yet another instance, I was sitting on the couch texting a friend when he walked in, he took the phone out of my hand and threw it against the wall breaking it. He then proceeded to grab me by my hair and started punching me all over my body. This time I attempted to fight back, but the punches got harder. At one point he got off of me. I ran out the door, running through the hallway of the apartment complex banging on doors, and screaming and pleading for someone to call the police. He chased me down the hallway, dragging me back in the apartment by my hair. The police never came. I lay there on the floor beaten, bloody, and bruised. As he continued his assault, I was so defeated…I begged for him kill me. I felt that low….I wanted to just die at that point. I should have left then, but didn't.

So the night I finally called the police and they can't arrest him because he left no marks, left me devastated. After all I've gone through, this can't be it?? Taking beatings for things like not giving him the remote control when he asked or because he thought I was cheating with another man.

I spoke to a friend who was a police officer in Maryland. He advised me that I could go down to the police station in Alexandria and file a warrant myself and have him arrested….I wasn't aware that I could do this as I wasn't advised of anything from the officers who responded the night of my call. I was afraid to go alone, so I took a friend with me and headed down to the station. There I met a nice officer, who after listening to my story, was willing to do what he needed to do to have my boyfriend sent to jail. He assisted me with writing a statement, which I swore to before the magistrate. A warrant was then issued for the arrest of my boyfriend and I was also awarded a protective order. My boyfriend was arrested that night and was released on bond just a few days later.

After speaking to the prosecutor, I was told it was a difficult case because all I had was my word against his. I still wanted to proceed. My parents came with me to court, my mother coming all the way from Florida. I bravely testified with him sitting there staring me down the whole time. After the testimonies were all said and done, things worked in my favor as he was found guilty. YES!!!! VICTORY!! A week later at the sentencing hearing, the judge gave him six months in jail. The crazy thing was I had been dating a murderer all this time, as I was later informed. Yes, he killed a man back around 1990 and served six years of a twelve year sentence.

During this time, I had moved back home with my dad and brothers. I was so uncomfortable there, initially having to sleep on the couch and just had an uneasy feeling about being there. I had escaped this place at an early age, getting married and living with my husband of ten years. Escape, an odd choice of words, but I was running. Talking to Dr. Dee Dee about my failed marriage and abusive relationships had led me to the root of my poor choices. I had tried to forget and bury it, but it was eating me up on the inside.

As a little girl, I had been molested by a relative. This unspeakable act came at the hands of my own brother, who was only three years older than me and with whom I was now living with. I remember him touching me starting when I was four and not stopping until I was at least twelve. I remember the smallest details, down to what I was wearing at the time of some of the incidents when I was very young…..a yellow and green swimsuit that tied around the neck…I remember waking up and him being in my bedroom, a bedroom I shared with my sister who is six years younger than I. And I remember telling my mother when I was about seven and I remember her not doing anything about it….why didn't she save me??? I remember…..I remember it all like it was yesterday. I was a baby…. Why didn't she love me, I thought…..Why wasn't I good enough?? I was so angry at her. How could she not put a stop to this?

The first chance I got, I was out of that house. I got married at a young age, running into the arms of an abusive man. He was physically and emotionally abusive, at one point beating me with a broom stick. From there I ran into the arms of another abuser. I hated myself...hated looking in the mirror, never wanting to be photographed, sitting in back during church so I wouldn't be caught on camera.

I had buried the details of my molestation for all these years, but all the while it was controlling my life. And here it was all back again.....all this emotion, hurt, and pain. I knew this was something I had to deal with in order to have healthy relationships. I cried a lot, and with advice from Dr. Dee Dee, I got in the word and started building myself up. I also started doing things for myself, like putting on make-up, eating right, and exercising to help feel better about myself. I would like to say that it happened overnight, but it didn't...I never gave up though knowing that the best was yet to come. I had finally built up my confidence a year later, and it was at that point that I was finally able to tell my brother that I forgave him for anything he had ever done to me as a child, whether it was intentional or unintentional. I also told my mom that I forgave her also. I let them go.....and I felt so free. I can't describe the feeling. Holding on to all that was hindering me, not letting me love as I should, and keeping me from God's best. Man, God's grace and mercy brought me through.... simply amazing.

I'm getting stronger in the word as the days go by and falling more in love with Jesus every day. I actually like myself. I'm still kind of shy....but I'm working on it. I'm most thankful that I never turned to alcohol, drugs, or prostitution like many who have dealt with similar situations. I trusted the Lord to bring me out and He was there with me the whole time....not letting me give up...causing me to win. As taught by my pastors, I'm living by faith.

And I live by these words..... "I'm not worried about tomorrow or the trials it may bring, for by faith I am the victor, I can conquer anything. I cast my cares at your feet and Lord you comfort me" (John P. Kee). Now you know my story. **SO What! I Am Still God's Glamorous Girl!**

Testimony #2

My praise is everlasting! My praise is lifted from the very depths of my soul! I praise God consistently, not only for sending His Beloved Son to die for my sins, but for keeping His Spirit alive in me even when I lived in sin. Growing up attending Church in Takoma Park, Maryland, and surrounded by the biblical teachings of my aunt in our home, seeds were planted. It is because of those word seeds, God's mercy, and prayer from family, friends, and Spirit of Faith Christian Center intercessors that I am alive today.

During my early childhood I absolutely loved church. In my home, if we didn't physically get up and go to church, my aunt would wake me up along with her four children to have "Children's church." There was no way for us to escape getting the Word of God. Besides, I never wanted to escape, because I truly enjoyed learning and hearing the stories of Adam and Eve, Jesus, Noah, Moses, Joseph etc. It was in those intimate family services that the spiritual foundation of my heart was being laid. And then I grew up...

As all of my aunt's children grew older, we became more and more crowded in the home we lived. At fourteen years old, my mom, dad, and I moved into another home with just the three of us. I was excited because I would finally experience privacy, something I never had growing up in a home with 11 people. At the time, my parents were not saved, so the door was opened for Satan to take reign in our lives. During my teenage years, the generational curses of my forefathers began to unfold in my life. Although I knew certain things were wrong because of the seed of Christ's Word that was planted within me as a young child,

I chose to satisfy the desires that were awakened in my flesh. After losing my virginity at only 14 years old, my self esteem, along with my soul, began to plummet into what seemed like a never-ending abyss. I felt as if I lost complete control of my flesh, and I began to die. {**Romans 6:23, says** "For the **wages** which **sin** pays is **death**, but the [bountiful] free gift of God is eternal life through (in union with) Jesus Christ our Lord."} Six years later I had not only lost my virginity, I had an abortion, abused drugs and alcohol, sold drugs, shoplifted, engaged in several homosexual relationships and even did so-called "exotic" dancing. Satan was performing some of his best work in my life and for a few years he succeeded. That is until some turning points…

In 2001, my mother became a partner of Spirit of Faith Christian Center under the tutelage of Pastor's Michael and Deloris Freeman. In my household, life as we knew it began to transform. As she began to apply the word of "faith" into *her* life, over time *my* life as I knew it began to change. In the beginning of this change, I absolutely loathed my mother. I began to blame her for every failed relationship in my life. I was crazy enough at the time to insist that she stop praying for me. I thought her prayers were the cause of my problems because she was "co-partnering" with Jesus to make me unhappy. Besides, I thought I was complete in my partying, my lustful lifestyle, and my relationships. Right? Well, as upside-down as that sounds, that is exactly how I thought before the gradual renewing of my mind began to take place. {**Romans 12:2**, "And be not conformed to this world: but be ye transformed by the **renewing** of your mind, that ye may prove what is that good, and acceptable, and perfect, will of God."} As the prayers of my righteous mom began to manifest, I began to realize just how miserable I was. There was definitely a void, a hunger that the women, men, drugs, alcohol and partying could not satisfy. I needed something greater, something more and something everlasting.

In July 2004, my best friend and I rededicated our lives to Christ at Dr. Dee Dee Freeman's Birthday party. Nonetheless, for me change did not come overnight and would not come without persistent obedience to God's Word. At that time I was still living in a lesbian relationship. Labor Day weekend 2004, I had just returned home from partying in Atlanta for *Gay Pride*. Soon after arriving home I had received a phone call that would change my life forever. The best friend that was with me at Dr. Dee Dee's birthday party had been a victim of a drive-by shooting and was brain dead. She passed away on September 6, 2004. I never felt so much grief, pain, and loss. We were like sisters. She loved me with the love of Christ and encouraged me to be the best woman I could be despite the fact I was living as a lesbian. I was devastated and there was absolutely nothing the woman I was in a relationship with could do about it. This woman took me to the Bahamas, bought me things and attempted to show me love the best way she knew how. Yet, there was still a void, and now that my best friend had passed away I recognized that void more than ever. On the other hand, there were some times I felt peace. These times were either at my church (Spirit of Faith Christian Center) or at my parents' house. It was where I continually received the love of God. It was at those places where I knew no void. November 2004, I made the decision to leave a lifestyle I knew in my heart was contrary to the Word of God. I humbled myself and moved out of the house, and like the Prodigal Son I returned home. To humble myself meant I had to let go of the pride which prevented me from admitting that the lifestyle I was living most of my life was wrong. I thank God for loving parents who like our Father God, welcomed me back with open arms of love.

I will not deceive you by saying that once I moved back home that all of the sinful desires I had immediately disappeared. No, I had struggles with fornication as well. It was like I was on a see-saw of sin, but unlike the playground of my childhood this was not fun. Because I was saved and sinning I was even more miserable than before. Day after day I felt nothing but guilt and condemnation for my unholy, unnatural, sexual desires. Finally, I prayed to God using these exact words as I would speak to a friend, (I did not use any *"thees, thous, shalls, or shall nots)."Look, I know you say in your Word that these things are an abomination unto you… Well, God it doesn't feel like it to me when I'm actually doing it… So, God I need to feel how you feel. Make me feel how you feel about it. I want to know what you feel, so I may forever please you!"* The next couple of weeks I was tested in the area of keeping my sexual purity with both men and women. It was to my surprise that I felt disgusted and detested each time. I was truly feeling how God feels as it relates to our sins. That's when I knew I was beginning to experience the manifestation of every prayer prayed in regards to my life.

I must make it clear that during this time of prayer manifestation there was a course of obedience to God's word that I had to follow. Being in tune to the voice of Holy Spirit by being immersed in His Word assisted me in transforming to the woman I am today. This did not come without struggle, yet my persistence to obey God paid off and each day life became easier. Finally submitting myself to the Will of God, I experienced the presence of God. In His presence I found out that there is a fullness of joy. {**Psalm 16:11**, "Thou wilt shew me the path of life: in thy presence is fullness of **joy**; at thy right hand there are pleasures for evermore."} And in Christ I also found peace. In the midst of trouble I was finally able to maintain control and make wisdom guided decisions for my life. My old friends couldn't understand how I just didn't "trip" anymore and why I was always so happy. {**Philippians 4:7**, "And the **peace** of God, which passeth all **understanding**, shall keep your hearts and minds through Christ Jesus."} That peace was familiar. It was the peace from my early childhood when I did not have a care in the world. Like Paul I became a new creature!

{**2 Corinthians 5:17**, "Therefore if any man be in Christ, he is a **new creature**: old things are passed away; behold all things are become **new**."} The old things and ways of my flesh were no more and I became the new joyous, Spirit-filled, loving, woman I am today. To God be the Glory! The Bible tells us in Acts 10:34 that God is no respecter of persons. This means that the same peace, the same joy, the same exciting, drama-free lifestyle is available for you too.

You must understand that this is a gradual process, so don't become frustrated. Your persistence and determination to overcome is the key! The enemy wants you to become frustrated; he wants you to give up and return to your old ways. Don't give him the satisfaction of having any more victories in your life and began to work the process. It is going to take perseverance, dedication, studying the Word of God, and prayer which is communion with Holy Spirit. Over the past few years, my life has done a 180 degree change, and I am happier than I've ever been. I yearn to see others experience that same joy and peace that is eternal when you are in Jesus Christ and walking in His ways. "Over the Rainbow" is my love offering to the Body of Christ. I am a walking example that Jesus can and will pull you out of homosexuality, drugs, greed, fornication, and anything else that is not of Him! Nothing is too hard for our God. He's just waiting on you to submit! {**James 4:7**, "Submit yourselves therefore to God. Resist the **devil**, and he will **flee** from you."} Now you know my story. **SO WHAT! I AM STILL GOD'S GLAMOROUS GIRL!**

Testimony #3

I did not realize I was "abnormal" growing up, until I met Chell.

She would always talk about her mom did "this" and her mom did "that" and I always wondered, "Where was her dad?" Well, she grew up in a single parent household and what made me "abnormal" was the fact that I was raised with both of my parents in the home... together! I watched my mom take care of the home (cooking, cleaning, etc.) and maintain a part-time job; while my dad equally worked (full time), to provide everything for his family and be the type of dad he did not have. I am the youngest of 4 children, and I did not understand how you could have 4 different children and have the same great love for all of them. I couldn't understand why we were not abused, molested, or abandoned like so many other children in my neighborhood. I was spoiled; if I mentioned it, thought about it, or asked for it... I got it! I did not lack attention, love, or esteem, so there was no need for me to try to find it in a relationship outside of my family. After dating this guy in high school, things changed. Like every high school relationship... you think this is the "one" that you are going to marry. He was cute, a great basketball player, and very popular- but he was also very possessive. He would convince me to cut class and have careless unprotected sex in order to show my "love" for him, because he was going to "marry" me. Well, all of that carelessness led to plenty of STD's and heartbreak, when I found out he was cheating on me. Each and every time we would have sex, I would go into the bathroom and just vomit and cry, because I felt as though something was being taken from me that was supposed to be a gift to my husband. I remember like it was yesterday, going to the doctor and hearing the doctor say I needed to take an AIDS test; that scared the crap out of me! I looked to God and prayed that if that test came back negative... I would remain celibate until I was married. I did just that. I became so focused on my walk with God and not in a man, that people would often ask me if I was even attracted to the opposite sex.

    10 years later, I thought the heartache was over when I finally met my husband and got married.

    It was a beautiful wedding, full of joy, peace, and love.

He was a very giving, caring, handsome, and a respectable man in the church. He "knew" the Bible. He was the kind of husband that all of my friends dreamed of marrying. After a few short years of marriage, I started to notice my husband would come home later and later every night. He began to hide his cell phone, emails, and new female "friends" that he worked with. He started to become almost obsessive with showering and working out at the gym. One day after being led to fast for my marriage, I began to hear in my spirit, "Something is not right." I began to walk around my house praying in the spirit and the force got stronger and stronger. Suddenly, there was a knock at the door and a female with a package said she has been having an affair with my husband for over a year. She described every explicit sexual detail of my husband's body and their intimate moments together. It was like something out of a movie. She had sexual text message logs, emailed conversations, even gifts that were given in their relationship. It took everything in my being to suck it up and forgive my husband and start the process of rebuilding my marriage. Little did I know... my husband had a different plan. We agreed that we would seek counseling and to my surprise, when we arrived at the counseling session my husband decided he wanted a DIVORCE! I did everything in my power to not cry, curse, scream, and yell. He just sat there and just threw me away, like I was a piece of trash and of no more use to him since he had gotten what he wanted from another woman. I picked my heart up off the floor and endured a VERY painful process of seeing the man I loved unconditionally live a life of a "single" man right in front of my eyes. I began to literally pick myself apart (my boobs weren't big enough, my hair was too short, my clothes were too frumpy) and every other flaw and every reason I could think of as to why "I" was the reason my husband chose someone else. At that moment, every insecurity that I had began to multiply 100 times over. I cried so much that I began to look and feel extremely ugly; I went into a temporary moment of depression. But one day, I decided that I would do and be the exact opposite of everything that the devil said I was and be the exact reflection of everything God said **I AM.** So, I got rid of every piece of dreary clothing I owned; I began to worship and praise God with my WHOLE heart consistently, and I confessed and placed a demand on God's promises that He would heal the broken hearted and bind up every wound (Psalms 147:3). He promised that would give me beauty for ashes and the oil of joy for mourning (Isaiah 61:3) and I believed that He would also restore (Joel 2:25) everything that the enemy has taken from me (confidence, peace, sound mind, etc); even the things that I had given him through lack of knowledge and lack of understanding. In marriage we are equally responsible for making it work and breaking it apart. I played a huge part in breaking my marriage apart by putting ALL of my acceptance, trust, and worth in my husband over my value, reverence, and confidence in God. I am no longer "abnormal" because my parents were together in the home, but **I AM…** considered a peculiar person, **I AM…** considered a royal priesthood (1 Peter 2:9) and since my price is far above rubies (Proverbs 31)… and in spite of every moment of heartbreak/ rejection, I confess and have decided **"I WIN"**-(1 John 5:4) no matter what!.. Therefore, I **SHINE** (Matt 5:16) with the presence of God. Now you know my story. **SO WHAT! I AM STILL GOD'S GLAMOROUS GIRL!**

Testimony #4

My story may be quite different from your average everyday "fairytale". Throughout my life I have made a lot of big mistakes, some which have cost me tremendously, I have lost jobs, cars, residences, and quite a few people in my life due to some terrible decisions that I have made. I've smoked weed and cigarettes, drank, fornicated, lied, stole, and the list may go on, but through it all, there was One who was there for me and never left my side, GOD.

I grew up in a family of majority men, all my male cousins and brothers. As I got older, I even took on a job in construction that was 95% dominated by men. So of course I grew up to have a lot of domineering ways and a very hard exterior. However, on the inside, I was just this scared, insecure, sensitive little girl that never had a chance to be just that. I was always expected to tough it out and hide my emotions and feelings just as the boys in my family were taught to do. This played a major role in my relationships and friendships. I have girlfriends that I have been friends with for at least 16 years or more only because they knew the real me. What was portrayed on the outside was just a wall that was put up to stop anyone from hurting me. It seemed that when I did put my guard down and let someone half way in, I would wind up getting used and hurt, especially by the men in my life. So this wall stayed up for years, and it even eventually spilled over into my marriage. No matter how I tried to cover it up, no matter how I tried to tear it down, no matter how I tried to go over it, under it, or around it, that wall was still there.

This wall interfered in my relationship with my husband and my kids. I wouldn't let anyone in, and I definitely would not come out. As a result, I developed a lot of inner anger issues, a lot of insecurities, and some unhealthy relationships. I couldn't let my husband love me the way that he wanted, because I was constantly pushing him away by starting arguments, assuming, and taking offense to every piece of advice or criticism that he had for me. My daughter wanted this "Mother/Daughter" bond that, at that time that I wasn't able to give to her, because I really didn't know what it was. I was never really a "girly girl," and I had never had a real relationship with my own mother. My sons thought that I was to strong because I was very dominant with them and not the gentle and soft female that they thought a mother should be. This was not only from being around males all my life, but because before my husband came into their lives, they had no father or any positive male role models , so I thought that I needed to be twice as hard because they were boys.

Harboring all of these unspoken emotions and anger issues throughout life led me to drinking, cigarettes, and marijuana. These were the things that would help me cope and deal with day to day life. My troubles, issues, and problems seemed almost obsolete when I was either high or drunk or both. No one could tell me back then that I had a drug or alcohol problem, because I thought that as long as I controlled it and it didn't control me that it wasn't a problem. My kids were taken care of. They had food, clothing, shelter; my bills were paid; and I got up every morning at 3am to work a job that inconvenienced me and caused me many injuries. I was entitled to get high or have a drink if I wanted right? Well, I thought I was. At that time I had no one in my life to hold me accountable for all my mess ups and wrong doings. Everyone that was in my life back then was doing the same things, so the pot couldn't talk about the kettle. As time went on, I was getting older, but my problems, troubles, and issues remained the same. Something had to change in my life and there was only one thing that I actually had total control over and the power to change, **ME.**

I started going back to church and reading my Bible, but I wasn't giving it a 110% like I should have. I would go to church and go right home and get high, have a few beers and watch the game. I would leave out of church, get in my car and light up a cigarette. I was a very luke warm Christian. I was only willing to meet God half way and play out the parts of His word that wouldn't inconvenience my lifestyle or the things that I wanted to do. I had to learn the hard way that when you trust and obey God, and want to live your life right according to His will and His word, it is the hardest thing that you will ever have to do. It takes a lot of self-discipline. It also requires for you to give up a lot of things and a lot of people in your life that you may not want to let go. Once I decided that I was going to walk this walk with God and walk it like it was supposed to be walked, I really found out who my true friends were and my real worth to them. But I had to continue to ask myself what was my worth to God. And not only that, what was I worth to myself? I had to be confident that no matter what happened to me on my journey that God would always be there for me.

As I continued my walk, my friends became very few. For the most part, I stayed in the house because I couldn't go to the place that I used to go and at that time I didn't have anywhere different to frequent. My day consisted of going to work, coming home, the kids, and that was basically it. After a while, it really didn't bother me as much as it did in the beginning. I felt like a totally different individual with a whole new outlook on life and what I wanted out of it. I was doing great, so I thought. While I was working on my relationship with God, I wasn't working on my relationship with myself. I still had my insecurities, anger, and emotional issues that had to be dealt with. But once again, no one was around me to bring this to my attention, so I thought that if I had God and was doing right by Him, according to His word, I was doing fine. I was doing way better than I had been doing a couple years prior; I had practically changed and rearranged my life for the better, according to me.

Then my husband asked me to marry him, and I was tossed into a whole new situation with new problems and new issues on top of the ones that I was already harboring. It was storm after storm after storm for the first couple of months of our marriage. We had already been through many trials and tribulations within the first few years of our dating. Once again, I thought I had conquered many of my issues during our dating stage. But we decided to move in together, and a whole new bag of tricks came along with that. It's true what they say, if you really want to know a person, you should live with them. The first six or seven months with us living together was hell on wheels. And not too long after me moving in, I became pregnant. We both already had nine kids combined, and we were both determined to break the family curses that we were definitely falling victim to. Neither one of us had been married before, nor did we know what we were doing or supposed to do. So this was going to be a learning process for us both. And boy was it; and it still is. Outside of all our fights and arguments, trials and tribulations, ups and downs, ins and outs, I wouldn't trade my husband for anything in the world. God had finally placed someone in my life that would hold me accountable for all my wrong doings and mistakes. He had finally placed someone in my life that made me realize how special and wonderful I truly am. He finally placed someone in my life that loves me for me and is more than capable and willing to take care of me and my family just as God intended. He finally placed someone in my life that reminds me every day of Who I am. I haven't had the fabulous life yet, but I wouldn't trade it for the world, because it has made me into the woman that I am today. Now you know my story. **SO WHAT! I Am STILL GOD'S GLAMOROUS GIRL!**

Testimony #5

I'm a woman that did not allow past tragedies to paralyze my growth as a Woman

Sitting in the dark again……. seemed like hours. Hungry, sad, and in pain due to the cowboy boot with spurs that was slightly cutting me in my back. The lingering smell of moth balls and various shapes of clothing on hangers, appear as monsters waiting to get me. "How can I make her like me?" I can't speak or cry due to the punishment I knew would accompany that act of betrayal. I remember asking God to be my friend and knew that He would not leave me alone in the closet. I was 5 years old.

Due to personal insecurities of her own, my stepmother made it clear that she did not like or love me. I was starved, beaten, thrown into a small narrow closet, neglected, and made to lie in someone else's urine for hours. I thought over and over again "What did I do? Maybe if I became invisible by not speaking, playing, or eating, I would not irritate her as much". Due to stress that a 6 year old could not comprehend, my hair began to fall out in patches. I received a terrible beating because my stepmom believed that I or my "friends" played in my hair which caused it to come out. I wondered to myself, "Is she crazy? Friends, What friends? Did she remember that she did not allow me to go outside to make friends? My only friend was God and He was in the closet!" Unfortunately, due to the breakage, my mom had to cut my hair very short to allow it to grow back healthy. As a six year old, I did not understand. I felt ugly and thought I looked like a boy. I began to view my mother as the enemy.

The brutal treatment, beatings, and neglect went on for years. I did not tell my dad because he was never around. He was too busy managing famous singing groups which required him to travel all the time. Besides, I didn't like him anyway. I felt if he was around, maybe my stepmother would not have hurt me. I did not tell my mom because I didn't know this type of treatment was wrong. In the 70's, abuse was not heavily discussed on television, school, or by your parents. As a pre-teen, I convinced myself that I had to be perfect and do any and everything possible to make everyone happy. This pressure caused me to develop a destructive rebellious attitude, targeting those that were close to me. Unfortunately, I lashed out by fighting, fighting and fighting. I would fight anyone at anytime but felt immediate remorse afterwards. Thinking back, I never understood the crazy range of emotions I experienced.

Throughout school, I was the SUPER STUDENT! I participated in everything from cheerleading, drama club, marching band, majorette, and the pom-pom squad. You name it, and basically I was in it. I was an honor student and an over achiever that consistently demonstrated the need to excel and be the best. Having the need to please everyone was exhausting for me. I felt unworthy to reciprocate any act of kindness which always left me emotionally bankrupt. I knew people genuinely liked me; however I did not like or love myself. I felt that I was never good enough. I suspiciously greeted compliments and kindness as a hidden motive to hurt me later. I built up a wall of protection that no one could penetrate. I was truly jacked up! I became my worst enemy.

Thinking that I had to be perfect became a huge burden for me and my family. Suppressing emotions which were planted as a child, manifested into an all out rebellious teen with uncontrolled anger issues. The holiday season was the worst. It took too much from me to socialize and pretend to be happy around family and friends. I began to alienate myself by not attending family gatherings. Seeking some type of relief, I would pray, fast and read numerous self help books to find solace or peace. I remember constantly crying out to God, asking Him to take this emotional "cancer" away from me. I did not like the imprint my character was leaving on the people I loved most.

I would awaken every morning to the paralyzing thought of trying to get through another day. I knew the Lord, was raised in the church, filled with the Holy Spirit and had the evidence of speaking in tongues, yet I had no joy……….I had no peace. I told myself, "Well, that's just how I am. I have to learn how to live with it."

In 1992, a friend of the family said that the Lord instructed her to invite me to her church. All I heard from her was Pastor Mike this, Pastor DeeDee that. My friend went on and on about how great her Pastor's were, assuring me that they could help me. I thought *"Help me do what? Ain't nothing wrong with me. I know that I have a habit of pushing people away and will tell you off at a drop of a dime, but that's by choice. Besides, didn't she just get saved? My friend is the same person that has beer in the fridge and was smoking a joint when I walked in the door. Whew........she had better get out, of my face.......and quick!" After keeping my cool, holding my tongue and getting my thoughts together, I demonstrated the manners my mother taught me by politely telling her "I'll think about it".*

That evening and all through the night, I thought about what my friend said. She spoke so passionately about her Pastors that I was intrigued. Sunday morning, I did not attend my church but visited hers. I'd never experienced genuine praise and worship honoring the Father so lovingly......so intimately. I thought, not bad…...so far, so good. When Dr. Mike got up to minister, I thought "Here we go. This man is going to scream, shout, spit, say nothing relevant, and get on my nerves". Well, shut my mouth and slap me twice, because that didn't happen at all. In fact, the opposite occurred. Dr. Mike's lesson was on the love of God. I felt that he was speaking directly to me. The word Dr. Mike ministered that morning pierced my heart and touched my soul. I cried throughout the entire sermon. I finally felt and understood that God loved me unconditionally. That was the beginning of freedom for me. What a beautiful feeling!

By attending Spirit of Faith Christian Center, I discovered that Dr. Dee Dee sincerely cares about the emotional and spiritual growth of women. She ministered at one of the Women Walking in the Word sessions that women needed to embrace womanhood by loving and appreciating one self and others. Her teachings and constant/consistent example of a Proverbs 31 woman ministers volumes to all to which I happily gleam from. I became a participating member, a consistent thither, and a ferocious intercessor. I absorbed all cd's, tapes and books necessary for my spiritual growth.

The abuse I suffered as a child was buried so deep that I had forgotten all about it. Having an intimate relationship with God, and operating by faith has allowed me to uncover and rebuke the hurt and pain that was buried deep in my heart and mind. I realized that I subconsciously held my parents responsible for what happened to me. The poisonous seeds that was planted as a child, no longer hinders my growth as a daughter, sister, wife, or mother. Praise God that He has restored every relationship that was broken.

I am a woman that did not allow past tragedies to paralyze my growth. I'm not perfect and that's okay. I can now say that I am happy, filled with joy, and have a purpose driven life. God did His thing when He created me………and I looove me!!   Now you know my story. **SO WHAT! I AM STILL GOD'S GLAMOROUS GIRL.**

Testimony #6

Have you've ever heard what you don't know will hurt you? Well, how about when you do Know and choose to ignore it…it can kill you! I know beyond a shadow of a doubt, that the choices I made in my life sent me on a detour, and the scenery wasn't all so great…

As a teenager I begin to resent being a Christian girl. Yes, I believed in God and church but His schedule seemed to be interfering with mine. I was sick of Vacation Bible School and having to leave early from all the sleepovers because my mom ALWAYS picked me up early for church. To me it seemed as my friends got to do a lot more than I, and they appeared to have it all. I allowed the enemy to trick me into believing that I was the one missing out on a great life, but what I really learned on this 20 year detour was, there is NO LIFE without God leading it.

I moved out early, staying anywhere I could feel a bit of freedom. I was tired of being dragged to church while everyone else got to do what they wanted. What I didn't realize is that even though I wasn't seemingly happy about being in church, the Word of God was still being planted in my foundation. I continued through life without so-called confinement, but for real my confinement was coming from me going against the order of God. The more I went along my way, the further I was getting off the path that was set up for me. Yes, I know now, that what God has for us is for us regardless. But…do you honestly think you have 20 yrs to spare like I did?

I was considered a smart girl with a bright future, but I also rejected being dictated to. My mom could say *right*, and I'd surely say *left,* just wanting to be let free to do my own thing. I'm still not quite sure what my problem was. I have two great supportive families. I was always popular and I knew I would be a famous hairstylist. Let me tell you, I probably took the detour just because I didn't want to follow anyone else, just plain STUPID! My mom always told me, if I put God 1st and made Him my priority,I would enjoy life more and be prosperous at it. Instead, I partied hard, was very promiscuous, became a single-mother at 20, had two by 23, and spent way too much time looking for love in all the wrong places. However, even in the midst of my mess, I still went to church. Even after moving on my own and so-called running from church, I began to want to go to church. I didn't realize that the Word planted in me is what sustained me through it all. So where I pushed away because my momma made me go, I now had a void there and began to miss the very thing I pulled back from. Yet still, I didn't get it! I was dating God based on my feelings. I was still missing having a real relationship with Him. Yeah, I know where all the books of the Bible are and could recite scripture, but did I know Him outside of my crisis? All my life I was a good manager. Oh, I could manage to get by in anything, but that was just sufficient. What happened to the girl with the out of the box dreams and goals? She was there but I had put her in confinement without realizing it. Oh yes, I had developed a great name for myself in the industry and was making what others would think is a lot of money. Yet, I still didn't feel there yet…mom continued to encourage me to stop putting my business in front of God so He could honor me. She told me when I did this, God would orchestrate my business to come to me without me being a slave to it and missing out on so much with my boys. To the outside I was living a star studded life, at the best parties with A-list celebrities all over the world….yet, I still wasn't there. A six figure salary, designer everything, world-wide traveler…yet still wasn't there!

At the age of 31, I opened my eyes and realized I went on a 20 yr journey, to end right back where I started…needing God! I call that phase of my life, which seems to be my whole life, MY DETOUR. I recall saying to myself, *"If I could accomplish and do all this Sherritta's way, how much more will I really accomplish doing life God's way."* I said that so many times until I took a real look at my life, and I realized even what I did accomplish was still by God's grace. It was the Word that was planted into my foundation that sustained me, that covered and kept me. See, I'd been placed in danger, seen and unseen; yet I was spared for such a time as this. My life was spared so much and I didn't even realize it. I was in a shootout and didn't know it. I was being investigated from being in relationship with a wanted drug dealer and didn't know. I was targeted by people who had bad dealings with my sons father, who knew who I was, but I didn't have a clue who they were. Jesus' blood covered me from countless attacks from the enemy on me and my seeds. So all that time I pouted about being dragged to church and rebelling for being confined at home, let me just say, I THANK GOD and my momma for my foundation! I know it was what kept me and the only confinement that was detrimental to me, was the limits I placed on my own life. I confined God and held Him up to move on my behalf, and yes I've now realized, and yet I'm still not there. Oh how I am rejoicing. I am not where I want to be but I'm sure NOT where I used to be, but my detour ends here. So now you know my story. **SO WHAT! I AM STILL GOD'S GLAMOROUS GIRL!**

Testimony #7

I knew High School was going to be a whole new experience, but I didn't know how different things would be. Leading a very sheltered life, I was only allowed to watch little TV, made to go to church 4 to 5 times per week, not allowed to go to parties or listen to the Devil's music and so on. I couldn't wait until this particular Friday night. Her mother had agreed to allow her to go to a home football game and 1 hour of the dance that followed, as long as her Grandfather was near. She called Granddaddy every day, just to make sure he was still going. He would reply, "I wouldn't miss it for the world."

The game this week was an important one. It was between two rival teams that had a lot of history. Our team was preparing to regain bragging rights, since we had lost by just a couple of points the previous year. You could feel the energy as you entered the stadium. It was like nothing she had ever experienced before. It was dark outside, and she wasn't on her way to church for a prayer meeting or in the house to watch Momma's "favorite movie" again; it was great.

The game was a tight one, but we won. Because of the trash talking, a fight broke out right after the game. My grandfather had left during the third quarter, because it had been decided that I could stay for the dance, as long as my cousin, who was a player on our team, brought me home. My friend got to him during half time, and he said that he would. Well, the fight got so out of hand until the police were called. They evacuated the entire campus. This put me in a very strange situation. I had nowhere to go. I asked a friend for help. She helped me to get word to my cousin to meet me uptown.

It was announced that the dance was canceled. Most people decided not to hang out after that announcement, and started to get into the cars of friends and family

After a while, everyone had left except my friend. She didn't want to leave me, but I gave a polite wave to her and her family as they departed. Deep in my stomach, I had a funny feeling but decided to ignore it.

"How you doing, Baby Girl?" asked the 6'2", 275 pound, senior linebacker, who we affectionately call "Big Jeff."

"I'm fine," I stated, as I tried to make myself smile. Jeff and I had a history of sorts. Our lockers were on the same hall and often I would find notes he hadwritten, or he would speak to me as I passed by. The letters were very flattering, stating how much he liked my outfit or my hair. Grandma had found one of the letters while I was visiting. She told me not to accept anymore letters from him. She said he didn't mean me any good, with him being almost 19, and I was only 13.

"Leave that grown man alone. He's thinking grown ideas that don't concern you."

"You're scared to death aren't you?"Questioned Big Jeff. "You know your Momma don't allow you Uptown." He replied with a laugh. "Does she knew you are up here."

"She's not going to find out. I'm just waiting for my cousin to take me home. Here he comes right now."

Coming up the walkway was Lena's cousin hugged up with his main squeeze. He and Big Jeff embraced and spoke briefly about the game and resulting events. After a little small talk, My cousin's girl gives him the sign to go. "Come on. We have plenty of time tonight. My mom doesn't know the dance has been canceled. Come on. Let's go!"

"Yeah, I'm out of here. I got to release some of this excitement," my cousin said with his award winning smile. He was chocolate with the whitest teeth. Everyone did what he wanted, when he flashed them.

"What about me, cuz? Aren't you taking me home?"

"Um, I really ...... Can't. Call your mom?"

"No. She's at church. If she picks me up from here, I'll never be able to go anywhere again. Besides, she's driving the Church Van tonight. She won't be finished until about 11 anyway. Granddaddy's at home and asleep. I can't call him either."

"I'll take her man. You go ahead and handle your business. I'm gonna have to settle for some food myself. I'll make sure she gets home."

"You sure you can take her?"

"Yeah, man. Go ahead. She doesn't look like she wants to wait much longer."

The two players embrace and me and Mr. Football are left alone. I watch as my cousin and his girl round the corner, at the end of the block.

"Aren't you getting in?" he asked already back in the driver's seat. "Come on, I'm hungry. That game took something out of me." I moved to the passenger's seat. Mr. Senior opened the door from the inside. I got in. The feeling in my stomach was still there a little, but it didn't matter. At least I was getting home.

"Can I go by the Spot on the way out of town?"

"Sure."

He stopped and got food. Now we're back on our way. The closer I get to my house, the better I felt.

"Do you have to go home right now?" He asks as we turn down my street.

"I probably should go home. Wouldn't want my mom to show up and I'm not there."

"Thought you said she wouldn't be home until 11? It just

a little after 9pm."

"Well, I guess, I've got a little time."

"Good. I need to go check on something just passed your house anyway. I can show you what I do on the weekends."

"Ok", she agreed.

As they passed her trailer, they noticed her Grandfather's truck in the yard.

"I didn't know Big John was going to your house."

"I didn't either. Guess he was making sure I got home."

"You'll be right back. This will only take a minute. I just want to show you something real quickly and then I'll drop you off. Ok?"

"Ok." I began to feel a little uneasy and that feeling came back in my stomach and kept getting stronger as we got further from my house. We travelled a few miles up the road and turned down a dirt path. Riding down the road, hundreds of times, I never knew what was up the lane.

"What's back here?" I asked.

"You'll see," he said.

We rode for a couple a minutes and then he began to slow down and cut off the headlights. We got to a section that was larger and he turned the car around, parked, and cut off the engine, allowing the radio to continue to play. I heard barking from behind a patch of trees. "Come on let's go. Come meet the dogs."

We walked a few feet from the car behind the trees where I saw a few beagles in cages. It was hard to make out how many because it was dark. He gave each one some attention and told them he'd see them the next day.

As we were walking back to the car, he began to remark on my attire. I had on brand new two-toned jeans, acid wash black in the front and white in the back. It was the first "hip" outfit my mom let me get since being in High School.

"Girl, I didn't realize you had that much backside. Those skirts you wear do not do it justice. You need to wear clothes like this more often", he said as he opened my door."

I gave him a polite thank you and waited for him to come around to his side. When he got in he told me about his hunting buddies and showed me the hunting rifles racked in the back window, which I hadn't noticed before that time. The conversation quickly changed to how attracted he was to me and how we should be together. Even though I kept insisting that he take me home, he kept trying to get close to me and getting angry as I declined his advances. Eventually, the conversation took a violent turn.

"Look, you're going to give me some tonight. I got all this stored up inside of me. You're giving me Blue Balls. You need to take care of this, before I take you home."

I was forced in the back seat and made to take off my clothes. The rest is a blur. The one thing I do remember is the final statement he made after he was done. He kissed me on the cheek and whispered in my ear, "You're a WOMAN now. This is our little secret, yours and mine. You're my woman now. You are definitely a WOMAN now." He took me home once I got dressed. I wouldn't let him pull into the driveway. I walked from the patch of trees. I needed the time to get myself together. What would I say to my Grandfather? My mother?

I opened the door with my key. Evidently, Granddaddy was asleep on the couch because my entrance startled him.

"How was everything baby?"

"Fine."

"You sure? You don't look ok."

"I'm fine. Just tired. I'm going to bed."

"Ok. Granddaddy's going on home now. Your Momma will be here in a few minutes."

"See you later, Granddaddy", is my response as he kisses me on the cheek.

"Granddaddy has such beautiful granddaughters. You're gonna grow up to be a beautiful woman one day."

"Um, hum."

"Goodnight."

"Goodnight." I said as I shut and locked the door.

I don't remember getting undressed and getting in bed. I just remember my mom checking to see if I was asleep when she came in and waking up the next morning. As I went to do laundry, I noticed that my jeans had blood on them. I tried all I could to get it out. It didn't work. I don't think I would ever want to wear them again anyway. I put them at the bottom of the pile of leaves in the yard before I burned them. That way I didn't have to explain what happened to them. "This is a secret………You don't have to tell anyone ………….. You're a WOMAN now."

It would be great if that was the end. However, it was only the beginning of a secret sexual relationship which got me out of my bed several nights a week and sneaking to the edge of our property. I could not hide from him. The trailer had turn out windows and he could lift my window and touch me with the barrel of the gun. Imagine waking up to that regularly. When I tried to move my bed, he would call my name, threatening to kill my sisters or my very hard sleeping mother if I didn't comply. He made me let him into the house and we would have sex on the living room floor. My mother never knew. She slept so hard and snored so loud that we would just alter our movements if it sounded like she was awakened. This went on for nearly two years. (I would only see him the second year when he was home from college on break. That was some relief.) Everything was wonderful until I thought I was pregnant. By this time I could have phone calls, so I phoned him to let him know.

"Well, if you are, it's not mine. I'm not even here most of the time. You could be screwing anyone."

I was furious. I asked him questions he knew the answers to, but refused to give them. He told me I wasn't going to trap him or try to ruin his life by accusing him of rape. He said he had proof of others I had been with, like his brother (my boyfriend), and I didn't want him to tell his brother how much of slut he was dating. His brother and I had not been all the way. We were in band together and the total sum of our physical relationship was tongue kissing and touching privates. He couldn't handle much more than that. He was definitely a novice.

I decided to just let it go. That was until my mother wanted to know why I hadn't asked for any sanitary napkins and there were none. I then had to break down and tell her the story or part of it at least. Once she found out that I had been sexually active, she stopped speaking to me. She of course didn't listen to my story, but called Mr. Senior. He told her just what he said he would and although I tried to rebut with the fact that I was raped, no one believed me, because I hadn't told them when it happened.

This was the beginning of the deteriorating relationship between my mother and me. She spoke no words to me for over two months. She spoke to me mostly through my sisters and by just making her requests known without directly addressing me. The relationship with Mr. Senior's brother ended for a while, and he started dating my best friend. When she wouldn't give it up, he came running to me telling me I owed him and if I loved him, I whould have sex. We spent nearly the entire summer on a daily basis being intimate. However, once school started again, I moved to a new school and he went back to my friend.

This started the cycle of feeling like I had to be sexually intimate with everyone who told me that they cared for me. Once I got a "boyfriend", we became intimate almost instantly. He only had to say the three magic words: **"I love you"** and he was in. It's amazing how you will accept affection anywhere you can find it, when you are not getting it at home. I think my mom was glad I was at school (residential high school for academically gifted students) and my dad was busy making a life with his new wife. I'm on my own. I guess I am a WOMAN now.

The lack of affection from family and self-control on my part kept this cycle going throughout high school and college. It's amazing that a major car accident, one week after high school graduation, requiring back, hand, and knee surgery couldn't keep me down. As soon as I had recovered, I was back at it again. I spent several years trying to figure out what I wanted to do in school. I didn't need to listen to my mother when she said "Continue in medicine," because she didn't care about me, but I did anyway. I guess I was trying to keep the "Honor thy mother and father" commandment when she forbids me to pursue Music as a career.

I was so overwhelmed with the way my life was going. I was in college, trying to work and go to school so that I can pay rent, continuously getting placed on the waiting list to start in my degree program, not having family support, and the numerous relationships. I couldn't take it anymore. I decided to take all of the strong narcotic pain pills and muscle relaxants I had been prescribed for my previous injuries. Thank God for friends and greedy associates. I was known in my building for cooking down home meals in the late night hours. I had called one of my kitchen regulars, letting him know that I wasn't going to be cooking. We were not physically involved; he was into guys. When he heard my message, he said I didn't sound right. He began calling me and sending people to bang on my door, knowing I was at home. They could see the lights on in my window. I don't know how, but I got enough strength to get to the door and unlock it, fearing the $500 noise violation fee from them banging and yelling outside my door. I collapsed, blocking the door, and it took a couple of people to push me and the door so that they could get in. Someone had called 911, and the police were on the way. I heard everything but could do nothing. The combination of the medicines and the affect they had on my body were more than I could fight. I listened to everyone around me speak of how much they cared and wondered why I would do this to myself. Someone called my mother and my father, both of which were referenced in the letter I was leaving. Then, I could no longer hear anyone. I knew they were trying to get me on the stretcher, but things were fading. I guess I was dying. I was finally showing everyone.

I woke up briefly to my mother telling me how they had cut up all of my clothes, but no one had been able to take my jewelry. She was saying how she was only going to hold it, not keep it, and it would be there waiting for me when I woke up. She also stated that I could wake up at any time because everyone wanted to see me.

I did wake up but I refused to see anyone. Following protocol, I was placed in a Psych Ward under suicide watch. That lasted until my father arrived. When my father came, I allowed him to come in. With the help of a mediator, I was able to ask my dad about the relationship between him and my mother. He refused to answer most questions. After the session, the mediator said, "I'm putting in for your release. You don't belong here. You need to stop blaming yourself for others' actions. I am going to require that you seek a counselor to speak to regularly while you work through these issues. You will also need some family counseling." Shortly, I was released. My mother asked me what I wanted to do. I told her that I needed a break from school. She allowed me to do so without arguing. My friends joked that my mother will only listen to me when she feels I'm going to die.

No longer in school, I had to find a new job. I needed to get out of retail. I took a short class and test to be able to get a job in the medical field as a nursing assistant. I primarily worked in a nursing home near the hospital. This allowed for me to get a better apartment (a 1BR instead of an EFF). I decided, after several months, to try to get into the nursing field instead of trying to be a doctor. I got into a program at a community college about 45 minutes away from my house. I had a new place, new people, new relationship, and a pregnancy. I'm really a woman now. Everything was great until I went by the baby daddy's house and saw him with another woman. He said we were through. I was devastated. I got stressed, started having complications, and had to decide to quit nursing school or quit working. I decided that I needed to work to take care of my child. I withdrew from school. Two weeks later, I had to stop working because I was threatening miscarry. Without having a sure way to support myself, and an infant on the way, I moved back home.

Upon returning, I was lectured by every woman in the family about how I was such a disappointment and how I was now a disgrace bringing a baby into the world instead of becoming a doctor. They wanted me to keep it a secret during the upcoming family reunion, dressing me to try to disguise my expecting belly. I was 5 months at this time, so it was rather difficult. We went to the reunion the next day. As soon as I walked into the house, I was given the look that reminded me not to let anyone know of my condition. My cousin ,who was finally pregnant after many years of trying, took one look at me and asked, "Are you ….?" I started shaking my head no, really quickly. She came over, grabbed my hand and said "Come with me, we need to talk". When we got to a back room away from my family, she whispered "Are you pregnant?" I just put my head down. She reached down and felt my belly.

"Girl, I'm so happy for you".

"I'm not supposed to tell anyone. I'm a disgrace."

"You wouldn't have been able to keep it from me, I've got pregnancy radar. I could have spotted you a mile away."

"Don't tell them I told you."

"You didn't have to tell me, I could see it. Even though

you are trying to hide it in all these big clothes, it's obvious. I don't know why they are making such a big deal about it anyway."

My cousin called for her sister-in-law and a couple more cousins came to the back as well. They remarked on the obvious glow they noticed when I walked in. Pretty soon, my grandmother came back questioning what all the secrecy was about. We said, "Nothing." She gave me the look again. My cousin spoke up for me.

"This girl is a grown woman. She's been practically putting herself through school and she hasn't once given you problems. Now, you're right, this is not how it was supposed to happen but it's here now. No need to deny it. You should be happy about the life in here. Not necessarily about the act it took to get there. Now come on, let's get these folks something to eat. I'm hungry." I was safe for the weekend around the family. When we got home, not much was said. I got a job and started preparing for the birth of my child.

About a month later, I was having some pain and I called my grandmother to ask what it felt like for your baby to drop. She said it was too early for that and if I had any questions, I should call the doctor. I did. They said I was feeling my ligaments stretching. Everything seemed fine looking at the blood work and previous ultrasound. They said it was normal and not to worry about it unless it was accompanied by bleeding or discharge. Then I would need to make an appointment to come in. Otherwise, I would just have to deal with it.

The next day, I was to go shopping for the crib and stroller with my new boyfriend. (Yep, still at it.) He was having some issues (alcohol) and called me at 4 am to call off our relationship. I got up and met him where he was to "talk things out". We wound up talking from 5 am til 12 noon. By this time I was starving and too tired to go shopping. We decided we would both go and get some sleep and talk later. I stopped at McDonald's to get a sandwich I was craving. I stopped by my mother's job to let her know that I was ok, since she left the house and I still wasn't home. She asked if I wanted to come in to eat. I told her that I was just going to eat and lay down. I got home, went in the restroom and it felt like I could feel the baby's head coming out. Home alone, and terrified, I grabbed the phone dialing 411 instead of 911. I screamed at the operator, even though it was my mistake. By the time I got the right person on the line, I was hysterical. They told me to take a deep breath because they couldn't understand me. When I did, my water broke. They sent an ambulance, but everyone around me said that it wasn't good. At 27 weeks, not many babies make it. But I knew this one was strong. Besides she was active and talented, loving music and dancing around inside when she heard it.

When I got to the hospital, they thought it was too late. To their surprise, there was still water left and the baby was fine. I was given the option to induce labor or to ride it out on permanent bed rest. I chose the later. After three days of bed rest with constant monitoring, I went in for ultrasound. The tech looked at me and asked if I knew I was in labor. I told her I had been feeling some cramps but they were mild. I also told her I hoped they would go away so my baby could grow more. This would not be the case. I went into full labor and gave birth (sort of) after 12 non-medicated hours. Everyone decided to take a break since I had been in labor & delivery all day. They left my nurse and went to dinner. A few minutes later, it felt like something kicked me. Sure enough, the baby's foot had slipped out. We went into super fast mode trying to resist the urge to push and waiting for the doctor, the nurse rubbing my daughter's leg to calm her. When the doctor arrived, he told me that she was coming breech and he would have to try to turn her to deliver. It was painful as the nurse and doctor turned my princess to make her passage smoother. One mild push and she was out. However, she took one breath and ended an exhale with a smile on her face. I sat up and watched as they gave my baby CPR right there in front of me. Unfortunately, that one breath was the only one that she would take. (RIP, my angel, October 31, 1994)

My first response was grief. I wanted to hold my daughter, who was much tinier than any baby doll I had ever held. She weighed just less than 1 lb. I sat there and held her and sang to her as we waited for the undertaker to come. When he got there, it still took me an hour before I could let her go. He assure me that he would make her pretty, although she would not be clothed (because of her size), she would be wrapped in beautiful blankets and the best coffin. I told him that I didn't have insurance to cover the amount. We came up with a payment plan and we had a graveside service to defer some of the cost. He spoke, I sang and read a poem, and it was over. It was all going to occur in two days after I was released from the hospital. Now I'm a woman burying her only child.

Two months after my daughter's death, I was planning a wedding. We would have a small ceremony at my grandparent's church with a reception at the community building where I worked. It was going to give me a spring into the New Year, all occurring on December 31, 1994. Now, all I wanted was just to have my father walk me down the aisle. We thought he was coming until that day. .... He refused. I had a nice day anyway. Too bad the relationship itself was short lived. He was looking for a ticket out. I was interested in moving somewhere that I could get a better job. How about Atlanta? It seemed to be the perfect solution to my recent problems. Find somewhere to start anew.

We moved in June and by July, my husband had found himself a new love interest. Her mother even stood up in the church I was attending and testified about how a wonderful man had come into her life, from North Carolina, and they were able to bless him with the room over the garage because his "roommate" had kicked him out. Of course, I set her straight at the end of service. She needed to know that the man she was talking about could not be her daughter's husband until he was no longer married to me. The next day, my husband, his new fling, and I met at Denny's to discuss our future. The result, she would help him get a divorce, and they would be married shortly thereafter. I was alone again, but still a woman. I showed up at the courthouse, fly as ever. Couldn't let him see he had hurt me, even though he had cleaned out the joint bank account. Good thing I had paid the rent and utilities for 6 months. I now had enough time to find a good job, to get back in the game.

    I found a good job, and subsequently, a new love interest. However, now I was getting smarter. We met in October, but we took it real slow, not becoming intimate until February. In between those times, I met people whose sole purpose was to make me feel better as I was ending a relationship. They really didn't want to have a relationship with me, I was STD and they served the same purpose for me. I had stopped going to church regularly during this time. I spent more times at bars and stopping by the package stores on the way home from work. After the rent ran out, I moved. Need another fresh start and less rent is always good. On February 14th, I invited my new interest to dinner. We had a lovely time. He brought my favorite wine and pink roses. It was a wonderful night. A couple months later, I was missing my cycle and took a pregnancy test after a long day. I crawled into bed with my new man before the time to read the pregnancy test. I was just going to lay for a couple of minutes. I woke after several hours and noticed that the test had two lines when I went into the restroom. It was a Sunday, and I screamed to the top of my lungs. He was startled and asked what was wrong. I responded that it was positive. He responded, "Get rid of it." I explained my past pregnancy and assured him that I would be fine if he chose not to be involved in the baby's life. I called my girlfriend, and she told me I needed to go to church. This is the point where I started attending services regularly and started really thinking about my life. I wasn't quite ready to fully commit, but I was definitely thinking about it. I stopped drinking totally and started looking forward to the future.

Eventually, my grandmother became ill and went on dialysis. She also lost her leg, below the knee. The doctors told the family that she may have to have an additional surgery to remove the leg further up, because of the lack of proper wound care. I decided to quit my job, and move back to help nurse my grandmother back to health. It was the perfect situation. I would get a free place to stay and raise my child and I would be helping a family member at the same time. I moved and in November, after a difficult pregnancy (diagnosed with an incompetent cervix that required a cerclage) my son was born. This was the longest that I had ever been without regular intercourse since the age of 13. For nearly 11 years, I had been sexually active. During that time, I had many partners. Unfortunately, if I was required to give an accurate count of how many partners I had during that time, I would not be able to do that.

During my pregnancy, I hooked up with a young man I had always admired in school. He was handsome, with an awesome smile, and a passion for music. He wasn't a musician; he was just able to talk about music. I think I was counting the days until I could be intimate with someone after my son was born. That was one of my best appointments, getting released to have sex again. We spent that night at the hotel. It was wonderful.

In a couple of months, I was pregnant again. It was now that I tried to convince him that we should be a real family. We started with the obvious things, getting a house, a new car, and yes, trying to find out the status of my divorce. It amazed me that a family that was so adamant about making sure they would marry had not finalized the paperwork in three years. I sent correspondence to them and asked that they speed up the process so that I could remarry. The decision would benefit both of us.

Unfortunately, the paper work had not been completed for the divorce, by the time my daughter was born. I had decided, as soon as I could get back to work and put away the money, I would do it myself. I never had to. Two months after the birth of my daughter, my fiancee got really sick. He fell out at work and had to be hospitalized. He would never return back to work and would be dead within 3 weeks. How could someone seemingly in perfect health, get sick and die in 2 weeks? Easy, he found out a week before his death that he was HIV+ and had full blown AIDS. He had contracted Pneumocystis Pneumonia, because of the state of his immune system and he had been without treatment for several years. He died on July 1, the funeral was July 7, I received my test results on July 8, 1998, required by his family to give up the house and car by July 15th. The diagnosis …. HIV + and my daughter was testing positive as well. She had gotten antibodies from breast feeding. We started treating my daughter and after 18 months of treatment and prayer, she sero-converted. GLORY be to GOD!

Although the world was doing everything in its power to have me give up, I pressed on. I went back to work as a nurse. Within two weeks I had reinjured my back trying to keep a quadriplegic man from falling on the floor. I had to have surgery. I immediately took notice and started listening to GOD more, reading the word, and asking questions. Social workers at the clinic were constantly trying to get me to spell out instructions for my children in the event of my death. They also tried to convince me that I would die without treatment. I actually did lots of research and spoke with the physicians which stated the contrary. I am closely followed with regular check-ups and to this day not requiring medicine (GBTG)!

On a spiritual level, the church that I had grown up in and where I was actively participating in ministry decided that I was sent by the enemy to attack them. (This they decided when my mother supposedly called them to ask for prayer for my "condition" while subsequently being informed of my inquiries of the traditions within the ministry.) I was told that my children and I must stay away from the leadership of the church and their extended family, and that we were not welcome there. I was told that I would die if I didn't stop my ways. So I left. My mother, unfortunately, but not surprisingly, sided with the ministry. Our relationship is still estranged. We may talk once or twice a year, and she will only invite the children to her house. Now, I am a woman, learning to trust and believe in God.

Shortly after being abandoned, I started a personal renewing that included complete fasting from secular music, movies, and television programs. I started getting disability since they told me I had permanent damage to my lower spine and I had to walk with a walker. I also pursued a degree in Music. Then things really started looking up.

I met a wonderful man. We were married. He led us to a church. Yes, this was difficult. We found ourselves testing every ministry we wanted to become a part of because of what had occurred to me in the past. We needed to find out the pastor's faith level on the healing of HIV/AIDS and their desire to have an area of ministry that would want to help people hope when given the "death sentence" diagnosis. We found a wonderful ministry where we both became active in ministry for six years.

I wish I could say that we had a wonderful time without incident, but that is not true. We've dealt with anger issues, multiple job losses, financial catastrophies, wrecked credit because of repossessions, homelessness, utility shut-offs, numerous affairs, many failed pregnancies, arguments, disrespect, and treating or being treated unlovingly. We've even had a legitimate reason to get married that would have been accepted in the eyes of God. But we made a choice. I believe that I serve a God that is bigger than what I can see or what people can say. We were advised many times to let go of our relationship. However, we have grabbed onto this crazy idea that our marriage is one that others are going to be able to look at, see the process and make their relationship better because they will have the ability to learn from our mistakes. We made a choice. And what is my definition of a CHOICE? I'm glad that you asked. A CHOICE is **C**ompleting **H**is will (God's) through **O**bedience **I**n **C**ritical **E**vents. Those events can be big or small and your choice can be good or bad, you decide. Either you complete what God wants you to do in the situation or you don't complete it. It cannot be partial.

I'm coming up on my 9th wedding anniversary (We never actually had a wedding; we went to the Justice of the Peace). I've learned the most about making my marriage better in the last two years with the most profound revelations coming in the last year. Here's a list of 10 things that I have seen help turn things around for us. This is just a list; you determine the order or importance.

- Sow into your marriage often.
- Get with those who have your answer. (Thanks Dr. Mike)
- Show love and respect
- Make the home SAFE.
- Celebrate the small victories.
- Love the God in him.
- Schedule time to communicate.
- Make daily deposits into the love bank.
- Remember, its about CHOICE!
- Disciple. Share what you have learned with others.

Remember, we are a work in progress. I am just allowing God to complete His work in me. Everyday, I might not always make the mark, but I'm still a woman, beautifully and wonderfully made. Now you know my story. **SO WHAT! I AM STILL GOD'S GLAMOROUS GIRL!**

Testimony #8

After two years of celibacy, I let myself down with one poor decision. It took a lot of effort to get to a level of spiritual maturity that caused me to commit to waiting until marriage before engaging in sexual acts once again. It took even more effort, which included therapists' couches, and repeated affirmations to build my self-esteem enough to realize I deserved more than temporary pleasure from unavailable men. In making this mistake, I thought I may have traded what God promised me for the so-called security of where I'd been in my past, but then Holy Spirit lead me to 1 John 5:18 and let me know that I belong to God and cannot make a practice of sin. I must remember I have the victory in all situations, even going back many years ago—a time when my life felt like one defeat after the other—I was under the protection of my Father, God.

I grew up in a home with one ill-tempered parent who was unconcerned with the will of God. The other parent was peace-loving and God fearing. The contradiction in their personalities certainly must have contributed to my own duplicity. I've heard depression defined as "anger turned inward," and I certainly dealt with my fair share of both emotions in those days. Simply put, I had no peace. I was searching for stability, calm, and love—I thought I would find these things in my drug of choice, men.

In middle school, I managed to lead a fairly undisrupted double life as I dealt with many personal challenges. On the one hand, I was consistently on the honor roll, involved in extra-curricular activities, and actively involved in my church. At the same time, I was also cutting class to have sex with a boy during school hours. I believe that most adults in my life at that time did not want to acknowledge the possibility that the young girl who paid tithes, taught children's church, sang in the choir, and occasionally delivered sermons, was capable of participating in such illicit activities. I continued living this hidden life into high school and the issues deepened.

Transitioning from an urban public school to an elite private school was brutal. I'll admit that I was quite the hot head back then, and the cultural differences between me and other students lead to many "near" fights. All I needed was to hear certain "fighting words" (disrespectful statements) and I was ready to go! Fortunately I had great friends who realized that fighting could have gotten me expelled and who kept me out of that trouble. However, they could not protect me from all of the trouble I would soon encounter, the sort of trouble which impacted me in ways that I could not know until much later in life.

My "first time"—classified as such because at the time I believed that not engaging in vaginal sex during middle school meant I was still a virgin—was during my sophomore year with a much older and married authority figure. He made me feel special and loved, mature and important, and a little mischievous. I'd become very accustomed to my double life and having such a big secret was a major driving force that kept us going. I told two of my best friends what was going on in order to have some sort of support system in case things became too much for me to deal with on my own.

During a summer program after junior year, I told one of the staff, but only after I swore her to secrecy. I needed an adult to share with; she kept her promise but I know she still regrets having made that promise before I told her what was happening between me and this man. We agreed that at the very least, I'd seek counseling to get help in dealing with some of my issues. In my visits with the school counselor, I talked about homesickness, depression, wanting to leave school...anything but my involvement with "the authority figure." I did not feel safe sharing with the school therapist as I worried about the potential consequences for him. I also was not prepared to really look at what I was doing and make changes, and so I entered a cycle of partial honesty with therapists that never allowed us to get to the root of the problem. I would later acknowledge as David did, that it is better to come clean with myself and God rather than hold onto issues. Psalms 32:3-5 (The Message): *'When I kept it all inside, my bones turned to powder, my words became daylong groans. The pressure never let up; all the juices of my life dried up. Then I let it all out; I said, "I'll make a clean breast of my failures before God." Suddenly the pressure was gone-- my guilt dissolved, my sin disappeared'. I had a few more steps on my journey before I'd release my life into the hands of God and arrive at the place of feeling peace.* The affair continued beyond college, before/during/after other boyfriends, through ups, downs, break-ups, reunions, beginnings and ends, right up until the last time I decided enough was enough and started to consider celibacy seriously.

In retrospect, I equate these experiences to a person struggling with a drug addiction. My drug of choice was the sensation of uniqueness and maturity that I felt from these encounters with men. However, none of the other men that I met managed to make me feel as special as I felt with "the first/authority figure". During college, I maintained ties with "the authority figure", traveling to see him as well as seeing him on his visits to the area where I attended school. I was open with him about my dealings with other men, of which there were several. Like a true addict, I tried various arrangements with these men in search of the ultimate high. This cycle was extremely emotionally draining, yet I managed to hold things together long enough to finish school and maintain friendships; however, there was a price to be paid for leading this double life. I knew I was getting worn out, and friends were concerned about the number of partners I had. There were late night calls, hanging out with men I didn't know (regardless of whether or not I had sex with them there were many times I put myself in some very compromising situations), inattention to my studies, and being hurt and broken more often than not.

The ultimate wake up call did not come until after college when life slowed down. Some friends traded all nighters and parties for nine-to-fives, others moved away, and casual encounters with men became less frequent. I found myself alone with my thoughts more often than I had even been in my past, and the "me time" meant I had less frequent need to keep up a pretense of "having it all together". I began to come to terms with my own fragility, and the reality of where my life was heading was so painful that I often had just enough energy to make it through the work day and would come home and cry for hours. I would sob all night long until I dragged myself out of bed the next day to repeat the process all over again. Realizing that things needed to change, during this time I narrowed down my involvement to a back and forth cycle between two "steady" men. I believe "the authority figure" and I were on the outs: still "friends" but not having sex. The "primary" man of the two "steadies" was deeply flawed, but I hung on to him for as long as I did because we talked about marriage. Through our relationship, I learned the hardship that was involved with attempting to have an actual relationship with someone who accepts their flaws, (especially as they impact other people), but does nothing to work towards correcting them. I had started the process of changing my ways and working towards being monogamous, but grew tired of waiting for him to change. Since I was not getting what I needed from either of these men, I decided to stop using the primary's behavior as an excuse to continue my involvement with the second "steady"; I called it quits with them both around the same time.

Before this, my tendency had been to keep exes around as friends, but I needed the finality of walking away from those situations. The second man, whom I met during my junior year of college, had made a decision to move back home to LA. At this point, we were not physically involved, yet it was comforting to have him available as a back-up. When he told me he was leaving, something snapped! I went to bed one night completely in my man-filled element, and woke up to realize for the first time in many years, I was man-less! This was not going to be my life- I was not ready or willing to make these changes. Before ending it with the infuriating one and the other moved across the country, I had set my sights on a very attractive man who was very involved in the community. Turns out he also had some very real emotional problems that sent even me running in the opposite direction! Around the time we had finally spent the night together (no sex), and things were starting to come together, he began to show his true colors. He was inconsistent, selfish, and confused about the message he was sending out and how he was actually living his life. At this point, I'd learned enough to recognize an unavailable man, and was feeling strong enough to walk away from this situation and not look back.

All of this walking away from and cutting ties with men lead me to the fork in the road. One option was to address the depression, the unhealthy cycle of relationships and the inattention to my spiritual needs. Alternatively, I could continue the road that I'd always traveled by seeking someone else to become involved with, suppressing how I was feeling and ignoring the warning signs of what I was doing to myself. I had not been actively involved in any church since the "super teen" days before high school. Since that time, I had received tapes from a church back home but rarely listened to them. I stopped paying tithes, and although I had visited a few churches here and there, none of them felt right. I somehow was not ready to give up the destructive lifestyle I had created. I always knew I'd get back into church, but I did not know when or how. When I would go home for long weekends or the holidays, I'd visit my mom's church with her. At one point, her pastor talked with me (during college) and warned me that I'd be back home if I didn't stop living how I was living. He and his wife would always ask how I was doing and ask where I was attending church. For years, they suggested Spirit of Faith and for years I refused to go and even visit, simply because I was being defiant. Although I did not visit immediately, I did not forget the suggestion. I was beginning to see that I was failing at life on my own. The Bible teaches that when a child is trained in the way he should go, when he is old he will not depart from it (Proverbs 22:6). I look back at the circumstances of my life and thank God that His word is inescapable; we must listen and obey (Hebrews 4:12-13).

With the help of my therapist --the first who I'd been totally open with about all my dealings with men, spiritual issues, and family life-- I began to take steps along the road I'd never traveled. It was through this process that I walked away from the two men mentioned earlier, began to take anti-depressant medications to help clear my head as I made these important decisions, started doing affirmations, and decided to visit Spirit of Faith Christian Center to take the initial steps to get my spiritual life in order. The first six months were difficult; I would tell myself (and others) that I was celibate more like it was a faith confession or an affirmation because I hadn't really embraced abstinence as a conscious decision. I felt as though the circumstances made the choice of celibacy for me as a result of recent events that had left me without a man to turn to for support. After three or four infrequent visits to SOFCC and deciding not to pursue any more relationships with men, I decided to trust God and submit to His will and purpose for my life. Proverbs 3:5-6 reminds me that if I trust in the Lord, stop trying do things my way, put Him first in all things, that He will direct my path. I made a commitment to God, SOFCC, and a life of abstinence until marriage and joined the church.

In the first year of my renewed commitment to Christ, God moved mightily in my life. Initially, I was reluctant to stop drinking and clubbing, but I desired to serve in Ministry of Helps. As I became more sincere about my love walk, this decision became second nature. I also realized there was no need for me to drink in order to be comfortable or enjoy myself. Dr. Dee Dee spoke into my life that I was coming off the anti-depressants in a year's time – within 10 months I knew that I did not need them any more and stopped taking them. It took a huge leap of faith, because I could not remember a time in my life when I was not depressed (without the drugs), but God saw me through it!

My life has steadily been on an incline since I rededicated it to the Lord. It has not been without challenges and setbacks. As the seasons changed from summer to fall, I began to sense myself feeling in a way that was a bit familiar. I would think "am I feeling depressed? Is this happening again?" Immediately I'd tell myself that was not possible and put the thought out of my head. I remembered what that was like and refused to go back to that place. However, around this time I had an opportunity to visit with the "authority figure." I had visited with him before during my celibacy and had been able to maintain it, so although I sensed that this time would be more challenging, I decided to ask a friend to come along and to move forward anyways. The supervised visit went well until I decided that I would take my safeguard out of the equation in exchange for private time with temptation. After you arrive at a place in God where you've truly learned better, it's not impossible to fall, but it is surely more difficult than it was in past times. I'm still disappointed when I reflect upon the mental process I had to go through to ignore the voice of Holy Spirit in order to continue on in that act. Afterwards, I felt such remorse and grief. I really began to understand what it means when we're taught that 'our lives are the greatest teaching tool for somebody else's life'. Although she never has said it, I believe my sister looks up to me as a role model for changes in her life regarding how she deals with men. I know my mother has given praise and thanks for the change in my life. Even friends who are not pursuing the life I have set after were rooting for me. There were so many people who would be disappointed by one stupid decision and facing this reality was almost paralyzing.

This is not the woman that I am now. Knowing this, I had to handle the situation differently than I would have in the past. I needed to remain accountable to someone and not sweep the incident under the rug. I also knew I needed to get some support from someone who was walking out the life that I wanted in Christ. I repented and although I felt unworthy of His forgiveness, I remembered that when we confess our sins, He is faithful and just to forgive us our sins and to cleanse us from all unrighteousness (I John 1:9). Next, I purposed in my heart to talk to Dr. Dee Dee about what happened. I did not know what I expected her to say or how I expected her to react. I never really had to deal with a disappointed parent before so I was terrified and ashamed. I told her that I had "messed up." She knew what happened immediately and I began to cry (again, because I'd been crying all day and had been able to stop long enough to call her). She was definitely disappointed but managed to encourage me to not give up and continue on in the things of God (James 5:16-20). I began to study my word with new diligence. I prayed and thanked God for forgiveness and new mercies. I filled my iPod with the most inspirational Vickie Winans and Yolanda Adams I could find and listened to it whenever I was not listening to the Word. I gave more energy to school—I did all the things I needed to do to ensure that I did not fall back into the old life and to push me to move forward. After a year of freedom from depression, I refused to go back! The peace of God is worth fighting for. I recognize that despite the fall, God still has a purpose for my life. I thank God that I can say, "Ok, I fell. I made a mistake, but praise God for a new day to let my light shine." I have learned from this experience, learned the value of living my life for Jesus, and remembered that He still loves me. Now you know my story. **SO WHAT! I AM STILL GOD'S GLAMOROUS GIRL!**

Testimony #9

I used to be ashamed about how I was raised in the ghetto streets of Baltimore city. The crimes, the drugs and the drug dealers were just an everyday norm for me. At the ripe young age of fourteen I became acquainted with any and every type of guy out in the streets who was committing senseless crimes or selling drugs to make a living.

By the age of sixteen I was dating some of the largest drug dealers in the city. Before I knew it, I was eighteen years old, living in California and became a hired drug transporter, transporting shipments of drugs from state to state. I did whatever I had to do to get the money and to keep it flowing on a continuous basis in my life. I was totally convinced that there was no other way to survive other than dating drug dealers and helping them transport their drugs for money.

I was now addicted to this lifestyle and by any means necessary I had to stay on top and stay in this game. If it meant putting my own life on the line, plotting with one drug dealer to have another one set-up and robbed for his drug stash and his money, then that's what I did. I wasn't fazed by anything. It seemed like at least once a month I would turn on the news and hear about someone who I personally knew or knew about them. Many of my boyfriends either popped up missing or were found later dead somewhere. This was my lifestyle and this was how I chose to live.

Ruthless and heartless I had become. I expected the drug dealers and the streets to love me forever. As long as the money continued to flow in and everything appeared to be on the up and up in my relationships with these men, we were cool. My life had consisted of occasional drug usage, sexual favors for material things and money, and a series of scandalous relationships. I was very bold and tenacious about this lifestyle, and I never thought that I could or would get played.

As a result of me dating these types of guys and operating with them in their drug dealing circles, my life begin to take a turn for the worst. I begin to do a downward spiral into a dark and hopeless pit. Without any forewarnings, I had become washed up and soon forgotten about. The same guys who were once calling me and chasing after me had now tossed me away to the side. When the money was gone, when the guys were no longer interested in me, I began to contemplate suicide. I thought that my life was completely over and that there was nothing else to live for. It was if Satan himself took me for a ride up really high and made me believe that it was all about me. He had me totally convinced that the world was all mine and then decided to drop me and leave me for dead.

When I had nothing or no one else to run to, I decided to turn my face back to God. It was then that God reached down, grabbed me, polished me up, and gave me a brand new beginning. It was a long journey back into God's graces. I really thought that I was big and bad enough to live my life without Him. Once my focus was back on God, He began to renew my mind and totally transform my life. The closer I got to God, the more He began to show me who I really was. I slowly begin to see myself as one of His valuable daughters. No longer did I feel the need to date drug dealers in order to feel powerful or special. The one thing that I learned through this whole experience was that it doesn't matter what you've gone through in life, you can always bounce back and have a new beginning. The thing that does matter is the people or thing that you let give you your identity? Turning to God and His word is what pulled me out and through to the other side.

I can hardly explain the joy, peace, and fulfillment that I am now experiencing with God alone on a daily basis. I am no longer wrapped up into this material world. I am now walking and standing in God's word and receiving His countless blessings in my life. I am a witness that God can pull you out of any mess, bless you abundantly, and make you appear as if you hadn't gone through a thing. All you have to do is turn down your plate on what the world is offering you, take GOD up on his **"WORD"** and walk it out. Now you know my story. **SO WHAT! I AM STILL GOD'S GLAMOROUS GIRL!**

Testimony #10

Choices. We live and die by the choices we make. Oh, how true this rang out in my life. Being a teenage mom at the ripe of 16 was very hard. I mean, for crying out loud, a sixteen year old with adult cares in no ingredient for success. During that time, I didn't know my tail from and head. Also, having a mother that I felt at the time was Cruella Deville in the flesh, impacted my situation the more. I often thought that I would wake up and this would only be a bad dream. Unfortunately, reality quickly set in. During the time that I was pregnant, it was taboo to be pregnant young. I had to endure ridicule, harsh comments, dirt looks, and verbal slander. I mean, people really knew how to hold you down. Through all of this, I realized I needed a plan, so I came up with one that I felt was satisfactory. My mom wanted to know what I was going to do. I felt great because I was a step ahead of her. I quickly responded and said that I had already put on together.

My mom said, "Alright, what's your plan?" (She did not say it nicely either.)

I began to speak, "Well, Mom, since I am still in high school and dropping out is not an option (she had stated this earlier), I plan to get welfare and food stamps until graduate. Then I plan to get a job."

Whew....a since of relief is what I felt for a moment until my mother snatched me up by one arm and said,

"Oh, No, Sista. You go it all wrong. You wanna be grown. Well let's be grown. No welfare or food stamps, suga. Grown folks take care of their responsibilities. You will go to school and work in the evenings, Grown Woman (this was her favorite name for me.) After work, you will come home, tend to your baby, and do your homework and chores. While you are at school and at work, I will baby sit , but you will pay me $75 every two weeks, Grown Woman. I am preparing you for life, because nobody is gonna watch your baby for free."

By this time I am in tears, pondering the thought of what was before me. By this time, my boyfriend, who is now my husband, had taken me to church, and I accepted Jesus into my heart. I was desperate for help. I had always wanted to go to church, but my mom never took us. Once I got saved, I thought surely my life would get better. In some instances it did, but in others it did not. I got some basic information about prayer, and I ran with that. I prayed a lot, and through this constant praying, I developed a since of "I can do." From that point on I realized that the very thing I was afraid to face I was doing it, being a mother. It was hard, but I was determined not to be a victimized teenage mom. I went to school every day, and I got *A's* and *B's*. I graduated with honors and kept my job at McDonalds. I did it.

I must say that my boyfriend, who later became my husband, stuck by me and took care of his daughter. I counted myself as being blessed because most boyfriends did not did not stay around, nor did they take care of their responsibilities.

Shortly after graduation, I married my high school sweetheart. He was my baby's Daddy, and out of that union four more children were born. My son, the only male out of five children, was a challenge from the very beginning. We really had to seek the face of Jesus during these challenging times. I literally felt forsaken by God. Now, don't get me wrong. I loved my son, but gosh, enough was enough. I started asking God what had I done to deserve the hell that I was facing. At this time, my husband was also tripping. He made several bad choices that caused our family financial hell. To add to this hell on earth that I was facing, my firstborn daughter decided that she wanted to experiment with homosexuality. I am now blown for real. During this time, I had to stay in the face of Jesus even when I did not feel like it. There were many times when I just wanted to give up and allow myself to just go crazy by focusing on what I saw and not on what God said. I was thinking, how much can one person take. How many times could I get hit below the belt. During this period, I felt like an absolute failure. I had failed as a mother, my marriage was in shambles, and my daughter, as well as my son, were tripping hard. I felt like I had every reason to turn my back on God because he had let me and my family down.

Even though I thought about turning my back on God, I never walked away because He had already seen me through much. I started calling those things concerning my children and my husband into existence, which I heard Dr. DeeDee say repeatedly. Shortly after I started doing this, I got a phone call telling me that my son had been charged with attempted murder on a PG County police officer. Oh My God, is all that I could say. This was another sucker punch. His bail was set at $500,000. All I could do was cry and pray because we had no contact with him. We knew no details. When we finally spoke and saw our son, he said the charges carried a life sentence. Trying to hold back the tears, anger, and frustration, I just stared at him. At that point, I felt like giving up on him. I had no facts, but I felt that I had done enough and had endured enough from everybody. I felt justified in being a victim. A victim of defeat and failure seemed to be a normal reaction. It seemed easy to give up and walk away from everybody. Even though the thoughts came, I had too much Word in me to bow down. When Pastor Mike and Dr. DeeDee talked about their son and his bout with the law, something rose up on the inside of me, and I began to fight in the spiritual realm. My son was the only boy we had, and I couldn't give up. I fought with the Word.

During his trial, they want to find him guilty and give him a life sentence. Not only did they find him not guilty for attempted murder, but he has developed a relationship like no other with God. What seemed to have been my darkest days, turned out to me my most victorious days, all because I chose to be a victor and not a victim. Our choices don't have to cause us to stay down and out. It is what we do with those choices, be it good or bad. Through all of this, I have put on numerous stage plays, and I am doing well as a wife, mother, stylist and play write. I did not allow these circumstances to stop my life. I chose to be productive, and I chose to win. Now you know my story. **SO WHAT! I AM STILL GOD'S GLAMOROUS GIRL!**

Testimony #11

We sat in the recovery room that cold Friday afternoon and awaited the news from my OB/GYN. Greg and I were having our first son after having two early losses, and were excited to become first-time parents. Thomas Gregory Sothern III (we planned to call him "Tre") was finally here! The scheduled C-section had gone smoothly, and we only got to briefly see our new baby in the operating room before he was whisked away to the nursery.

As the doctor approached, I was waiting for her to tell us when they would bring our new bundle of joy, but as I looked at her eye, I detected a look of concern. With the most comforting voice she could muster, I heard her tell me through my morphine-induced haze, "Well, I have good news! The good news is, the baby's heart is strong."

Okay, so what? I thought. Isn't it supposed to be? I had not expected anything less. She could sense that we were expecting her to say more, so she went on, "Your baby has arthrogryposis multiplex congenital ..." and as she continued to talk her voice transformed to a whir of white noise. What? What in the world? How could this be? I could hear her voice in the background and I could distinguish phrases like, "Most kids have a good prognosis," "Lots of therapy, splinting and braces" and "Several surgeries." My thoughts tumbled together like the clothes in a clothes dryer and I struggled to come to terms with what that meant. So – this is our first son. Will we be able to do this? Will I be able to continue my job as a teacher? As she continued to talk, she gave us a stack of papers with information on websites and support groups that would give us more background knowledge of the disease and some idea of what things we should expect with a child who had such great needs. The clothes in the dryer turned into pins and the noise in my mind was deafening.

Greg (I think) spoke up first, "So, when will we get to

see him?"

"The pediatricians are working with him now to get his breathing stabilized. He'll be transferred to Children's Hospital, but I'm going to make sure that you get to see him before he gets transferred out."

She left us to make sure I was put into a room that would allow us privacy with the baby. As she walked away, we looked at each other with a million questions in our eyes. I immediately burst into tears.

My husband embraced me, and letting his own tears fall, he reminded me, "Okay, you know what the Word says about this situation. He is healed by Jesus' stripes. We have already covered him with our prayers and the blood of Jesus. We just have to wait for his body to line up with what the Word says. The words of our pastor Dr. Mike Freeman and his wife Dr. Dee Dee Freeman echoed in my mind and were being replayed like a recording, "If it's in your life, you can handle it ... God is able to do exceedingly abundantly above all you can ask or think ... we having the same spirit of faith, according to as it is written, 'I believe, therefore have I spoken, we also believe, and therefore speak!' " They had poured those words into our lives over the years, and we were being forced to draw upon that Word like water in a well. It was nourishing, replenishing, and it has continued to support us throughout our lives.

My mother, mother-in-law, and aunt (who had all been waiting throughout the procedure) came in the room and surrounded us with their love and encouragement. My aunt reassured us, "God knew that you all would be wonderful parents, and that He could trust you with this special baby." I heard her words with a twinge of resentment. Sure, I had sown into the lives of hundreds of children over the years as a Youth Department worker, a Kindergarten/First Grade teacher, and as a "big sister/auntie/godmother" to so many others. But shouldn't that mean that when it is my turn, I should have a healthy baby of my own? If I have sown, shouldn't I also reap – that's what the Word says, right? Why is it so easy for many and so difficult for me? I wasn't sure I wanted to be "trusted" with a "special baby."

Later on, they wheeled my tiny little baby boy into my room in an incubator. His skin was pink and his black thick hair peeked out at me under a blue and pink cap. I gingerly rubbed his arms through the holes on the sides of the incubator, and the transport team seemed anxious to get going with him. The transport nurse gave us information for the neonatal intensive care unit (NICU) at Children's National Medical Center in Washington, DC and assured us that they would take good care of him, and we could come to see him as soon as we could. Then he was gone, and I was left on the maternity ward with empty arms that ached for my baby boy. Later that evening, Greg went to the hospital to be with the baby while I was still confined to my room, and he spent the weekend splitting his time with me during the day, and with Tre' at night.

That Monday I was released from the hospital and Greg and I drove immediately across town to see Tre'. His team of physicians knew we were coming and were awaiting our arrival. When I approached the isolette I noticed that there were no other babies in his room. The monitors and machines were blinking and beeping and doing their thing. And I saw him – I mean fully for the first time. His feet were twisted up and his legs were bent like a pretzel. His tiny little fingers were so tight that you could not pry them open with your pinkie finger. His chest rose and fell to the rhythm of the ventilator, and his eyes were shut tight. His muscles were flaccid and he did not have the routine movements that one would see in a newborn. His body was so diminutive in such sharp contrast to the massive machinery around him that was supporting his life. The doctors, who had stepped back to allow me my moment, asked for permission to approach, and through my tears I told them to come. They peppered me with questions about my pregnancy – was it full term? Yes. Did you feel him moving? Yes. Do you have any history of such in any immediate family members? No. Are you and your husband blood relatives? No (they had to ask). After what seemed like an hour, the geneticist explained to me that Tre' had not moved in the womb and because he was immobile for so long, it caused his joints to become contracted and stiff. He had no gag, suck, or swallow – reflexes that are present in typically-developing newborns. His muscles were very weak, and because the different organs in his body are muscle (like the lungs) they were weak also.

They did not yet have an explanation as to why his body was having this challenge, but they wanted us to be prepared for intensive care and support. They surmised that he would probably not move, breathe or eat on his own. He would probably have to be institutionalized, and he might possibly have a very short life-span. This, of course, was unacceptable in our minds, and we could not allow the possibility to take root in our thought or belief system. We immediately went into warrior mode. We prayed over him every day. Our church family, intercessors, and leaders prayed for him. My in-laws had their church members praying for him, and even the missionary in Guatemala, who was affiliated with the family, had the children at her orphanage praying for him. The mother of one of my students had her church members put him on a 24 hour prayer watch for a month. There was too much promise, too much faith, and too much Word spoken into the life of that baby boy to let what the doctors were saying to come to pass.

Six years, dozens of surgeries, hours of therapy, and untold time spent in Children's Hospital later, Tre's life has been a demonstration of God's healing power to all. He is walking, talking, and eating independently. He loves music and sings all day long (his teachers are trying to get him to stop!) He is a Kindergarten student who is reading above grade level, even while being in a special education classroom setting. He still has a long road ahead of him, but he has been able to confound the doctors who had once said he would be confined to his bed for the rest of his life!

And me? While I was once a more timid "crier," I have learned to become a fighter. I have had to learn to operate in faith and believe the promises of God in spite of what the "experts" have told me. I have had to lean on the love and support of my biological, church, and work families; and I have learned that God always provides us with people in our lives who will use their power, their ability, and their influence on our behalf. And in spite of having and losing another son after 37 weeks when Tre' was two years old, I am proud to say we now have yet another son who has absolutely no physical challenges whatsoever! I learned that after all that I had sown, I was entitled to reap – but in ways that I never would have imagined before having Tre'. And I have been able to take our situation and use it as a testimony to so many other women and families who have had similar challenges in life. Being able to press on in spite of these difficulties and bless the lives of others with my story has been my greatest victory. Now you know my story. **SO WHAT! I AM STILL GOD'S GLAMOROUS GIRL!**

Testimony #12

November 8, 2009 was my Resurrection Day. Every day prior to that, my life was filled with torment and torture from the enemy. I was deceived into thinking there was something wrong with me mentally but too ashamed to share my darkest secrets because of my self-consciousness. For more than half my life I struggled with depression. My earliest memory was about twelve years old. I despised my outward appearance so much, that I used food to comfort me. As my weight increased, I became more self-conscience and ate less and less. I didn't have many people to talk to, and as much as I loved my family, I'd always felt out of place around them. My father was always angry about something, my mom was always hiding behind her "rose-colored glasses," and my sister was away at college.

As I got older, it seemed as if my depression got worse. In high school, I remember on several occasions burning myself with a hot curling iron because I was so disgusted with myself. If I'd failed a test, didn't do my homework, or got into trouble, my own punishment was worse than my father's discipline. Many times I just wanted to die. I tried, but I could never go through with it. Each time I thought about how my mom would feel, and I loved her too much to disappoint her.

When I got to college, I was determined to put everything behind me and start over; and I did my freshman year, at least so I thought. I'd made new friends and had a good time, but my depression was far from over, and to make matters worse, loneliness started to set in. My grades started to slip, and my GPA nearly plummeted; so I took a semester off and joined the military. I figured I needed the discipline and the military was a perfect start. It was scary but exciting at first; however, shortly after arriving to basic training, my depression reared its ugly head. As I tried to find myself, I researched different religions, hoping to find one to meet my needs. I'd grown up in a traditional Baptist church and had some knowledge of the Holy Trinity, but not salvation. As I studied the different religions, I never found one that sat right within me, so I ended up walking away empty handed.

After my training was over I went back to college. My whole life up to this point was like living in a mental jail cell. With each new thing I tried, the cell door appeared to be unlocked, or so I thought. I now realize I was using the wrong key. At the time, however, I was stuck like chuck because I was too ashamed to share with others what I was going through; and the only person who truly knew, my best friend, was two hours away at college. The only thing that made going back to school different was that I got saved. I'd always knew there had to be more to life than how I'd lived it and I just knew my salvation was an answer. I figured once I got saved, everything would gradually change, automatically. My depression would finally come to an end, and I could finally be happy and joyful. I immediately starting attending a church and became active in different ministries, but my depression was still far from over. I'd praise God during choir rehearsal and Bible study. Then I'd come home as if nothing ever happened.

Still not recognizing the root of my problem, I decided to move to Maryland, where a few friends introduced me to Spirit of Faith Christian Center. Almost immediately after joining, I backslid and stopped attending service and Bible study. At one point I got so depressed that I began to literally question God about why He created me and continued to allow me to live. In the fall of 2009, I went to church and Pastor Mike was preaching about the things we bind on Earth, God will bind in heaven. And shortly after, November 8, 2009, I declared my depression as being over and absolutely refused to allow it back into my life. There have been a few occasions afterwards that I've felt saddened and wanted to give into my feelings, but I remembered what I spoke and to give in would have made me a liar; so I prayed. The more I prayed and drew closer to my Father, the smaller my image of Satan became. While I was in the middle of my mess, he resembled a huge force that I was a slave to; he was too big for me to fight, so I gave in and lived life feeling defeated. But God! My Father, always reminded me how much He loved me, whether through the beauty of the fall leaves changing or by whispering in my ear while I walked through a park. He never kept His adoration of me a secret. And the greatest key to my overcoming depression was having the understanding of walking by faith from my pastor. It was by faith that I made my declaration and it is by faith that I continue to walk in new freedom. Now you know my story. **SO WHAT! I AM STILL GOD'S GLAMOROUS GIRL!**

Testimony #13

Now it's really time to go there. You know where it is. We hear it on television all the time, "If I can make it there. I can make it anywhere. It's up to me New York, New York." This is all I can remember hearing as I stared gazing, trying to live my life through the picture screen most of the time. I just wanted to go there. I had enough of being punished all the time and being called "the Church Girl" by my so-called friends. Well, today I've had it. If my mother thinks she is going to tell me that I can't go to Emerson College Preparatory, she can forget it. In fact, forget her, forget them all.

    I had taken many whippings over the years. Nothing I did made sense or was ever good enough. My vice principal told my mother that my scores were on a college level and going to Woodrow Wilson would not be challenging enough for me. I thought it would be great since it was the only International Public School in DC. My Aunt Millicent and Uncle Carlos went there, and my mom looked up to them. However, Mrs. Brattick still said it wasn't enough for me. I needed more to keep my mind stimulated. Who did she think she was, having me research schools at the age of 13, to find the ideal one not too far from my house. Hey, the school I wanted, Woodrow Wilson, was a ten minute bus ride away. Now that was convenience. One of my mom's friend confirmed that I wasn't dumb. She said that my rebellion stemmed from the fact that I was just not being challenged. I thought to myself, who wants to give up the title as the "class clown" to do work.

    A friend of the family sent one month's tuition for me to go to school. He said that he believed in me. Tuition was going to be steep! So help had to come from somewhere.

My mom had been saved now about eight years, and she had been in faith churches. When she wasn't working, she told me we had to live by faith. This same faith that would cause people to leave grocery bags on the front porch, had me expecting to go to a school since someone had sent the first month tuition of $1300.00. I don't even think we had the lights on consistently. That didn't matter because I was already being ridiculed in so many circles about what I had and especially about what I didn't have. All I remember is that she told me the money was for me to go to school.

Well, that was it. At the last minute before the new semester began, my mother told me she wasn't going to be able to pay for me to go to school. I remember sitting beside her in the bathroom while she bathed, where we had our normal talks. I just calmly got up, packed my things, went into her wallet, and took the two $500 money orders and $300.00 in cash. I thought, well, this was for me to go to school, so it belonged to me. Later I found out that my mother had pressed charges against me. I believed this messed me up when I finally came back from Job Corps. It was very selfish of me at the time. I know that while you're reading this, you must be thinking, what kind of daughter would steal money from her non working mother? I don't know, but I did do it.

Off into the world at almost 14, I was going to NYC to make a name for myself. My mother was going to eventually get the money back. I just needed some start up capital. Well, the money orders were in her name, so I couldn't cash them. She actually got the money back. All over DC before I left, I tried to cash them, but to no avail. Finally I boarded a bus going to Time Square and I was out of there. Arriving in NYC, I wasn't afraid, because when you are as young as I was and had already known what it was to be with a man for several years now, you coulf spot all the predators wherever you went. I felt like I had made it to my own Emerald City, and I was off to find my Wizard. Not too long after arriving and gorging on my own lust and appetites for things (clothes, jewelry), my money had depleted.

Walking through Broadway and then hopping on and off trains all night began to take its toil on me day after day. I suddenly realized what I could do after talking to one of the ladies I had come across. I had been molested for years, so I was by no means interested in having sex with anyone. In fact, I was deceived into believing if that had not happened to me, maybe I would have waited until marriage. Well, one sure way to make money was to become and exotic dancer (stripper). It was actually so exciting for me because I already at a young age had an understanding of the perverted heart of men's lust and their desires. Older men love young girls. As of this day, I have been married three times to men older than me by 7-17 years. My thinking was if I could some how pay all the men back for what had happened to me as a young innocent child, I would be settling the score and teaching them a lesson.

I always thanked God for the glass window that separated me from the men as they watch me day after day. They were only supposed to look but could never touch, or so I thought! Oh, I was good. Sin had me thinking I was one of the youngest things on Broadway. That was just the beginning of my enthusiasm for all kinds of genre of music that was popular in that age and time. That music would transform me and stir up some of the most sensual moves to entice the men, and they kept coming back. Eventually, it happened much like I dreamed it would happen. The lead actress would become sick, and I, the diligent understudy, would have to step in and play the role. Then everyone would get to see how great an actress I was.

Actually, the call that came was because the headliner at club 711 couldn't make it and they needed me Kit Kat, my chosen stage name from my favorite candy bar. Down Broadway I ran in heels, a wig, lingerie, and a trench coat. To finally become a headliner was a dream come true. I had a 15minute gig every hour from 8pm –3am. You couldn't beat that, $800.00-$1400.00 a week during the ages of 13-16 years old. It was the most exciting thing I had ever done. I had my name in lights on Broadway. One day that will happen again, but it won't be from stripping.

By now I had gotten myself a little apartment, not too far from the strip, and I would think to myself that if I could go down to either Penn Station or Time Square, perhaps I could spot the other runaways before the predators got them. I didn't understand that the responsibility of being the oldest child, I instinctively took the role being protector and provider. Many young ladies came through my apartment, and I would give them the choice of either staying or going back home. Looking back, most of them chose to go back home, after I would talk with them and give them a glimpse into the life I was leading. I would explain to them that It really wasn't all glitz and glamour like I thought it would be. It was hard work to keep a man off the top of me and trying to hump my lights out. Eventually, all roads would lead to the one thing that you feared the most, which was living a life of a prostitute.

The dreadful day finally came when the laws were changing, and I had to go to the Bureau of Vital Statics and get my birth certificate to prove that I was actually 18, and not some minor that this club had been exploiting. I couldn't show proof, so I had to retire. I figured that I would just go to another club. Surely they had heard of "Kit Kat." Oh, they had heard, and the word around that 12 block radius was that she can't produce documents; she must be a minor; "keep her out the clubs." So rents going to be due, and I have another new young lady depending on me to get her a bus ticket to get home. We have to eat. What am I going to do? Instinctively, the only thing I knew to do when my sisters were hungry back in DC would be to sell my body to some Joe for a few minutes for a whole lot of dollars.

I remember when this Caucasian guy came up to my

place. The whole time I had been in NYC, not one male had been to my place except for repairs. Here he comes through the door. I thought this was going to be quick and easy. Hey, I had convinced him to pay me somewhere between $300.00 -$700.00, but once wasn't enough for him. He was some big shot with money, and by the time he left, I had $1700.00. Well, I was just glad that I didn't get killed because girls were dying around that area like flies, and I didn't want to become a statistic. I took care of everything I knew to take care of. I got the young girl her bus ticket, and once she left me, I prayed that she would make it back home to her parents.

I didn't want to have to live my life as a prostitute. So after some early morning walks and some soul-searching, I humbled myself, like the prodigal son I had so many times read and heard about all of my early years in church, and called my family to pick me up. I recall ducking them a couple of times that they came to look for me. Now it was time to let go and go home. But how does a teenager who has done as much as I did (the way my mother would say it) really ever be able to come home and just be a kid again.

Well, it wasn't easy. There were many more hiccups down the line, but after all the residue of sin left I finally decided I wanted more out of life. I eventually got a respectable job, making respectable money; however, I couldn't get the relationship factor down to a science. I went from boyfriend to boyfriend and eventually husband to husband. After finding out some really bad news regarding my husband's behavior, I decided to really let God into some other areas of my life. From all the molestation and all the different sex-partners, I was carrying quite a bit of baggage.

I was really deceived by the enemy into believing that God didn't care about that part of my life. See, the way I saw it at that time, once I got married, I had a license to have sex for the rest of my life guilt-free. Yeah right, if I could just get it in the right time period, maybe that would have been true. Although, I would have such good sex before I got married, I was really bored by the time it was the right time to enjoy my mate. Since I had already given out so much of myself before my husbands, my tolerance for them was very thin. Well, by my third husband, I had accepted what my pastors had declared, "Marriage is till death do you part."

Even still, I was so miserable, I wanted him to die. I would be hoping that the train would derail on his way home, or he would get in an accident at work. Then he would walk through the door, and I just figured he got away again from death. Oh the days I wept like Esau, believing that I had done that irrevocable thing when I married, and to this day it almost was true. When I made up my mind to be and do and act like the wife God had called me to be, I then saw for myself what was causing so much misery and pain and sleepless nights. When the sin was exposed, I feared after a life of such unfaithfulness that I would cheat on him; but God's grace kept me, so I wouldn't let go.

We eventually split because of all of the three A's he was committing, adultery, abuse, and addiction. I thought that my life was over. It wasn't as easy as I thought it would be without him. I dismissed the prior two husbands like a miser would a bank withdrawal slip. It was no problem at all when it came to them. Although he was the one I wanted to get rid of, he was the most difficult one to get over, oddly enough! Well, during this time of separation while awaiting the divorce, the hand of God, of course, was at work as usual, in my life orchestrating things.

Earlier that year my first lady and mother in the faith, Dr. DeeDee Freeman, hosted her quarterly Women Walking in the Word meeting. When we came in to be seated, we were given a piece of paper which said, "Dreams really do come true." Well, she wanted us to put down our top three dreams that we were believing for. Well, I was excited that I put down my three and believed God for them right then and there. Then I got an extra sheet, so I could leave one in my Bible to reflect on during the wait time, while she and staff would pick the winners. Well, that was in January of 2009. By the end of April 2009, I was separated from my husband. Between May and July of that year, I was notified that I was the lady who Dr. Dee Dee had chosen to make her dream come true.

God the Father is the greatest example of His order and the way He has His principles set up. It is a known fact that whenever you take something from your child that you believe and know is not profitable or a danger to them you must replace it with something of better value than what is being removed. For example, you want your child to stop listening to so much of the secular music, but you don't share or turn them on to any cool Gospel. You don't want him listening to so much Lil Wayne or T-Payne, but you didn't buy him/her any Canton Jones or T-Bone, so that he can still get his chill time on and get ministered to at the same time. It's got to be a better exchange, like God giving one Son so that in exchange He could inherit many sons.

Well, my exchange from my Big Daddy God was the 23 years I had not heard or seen my father of whom I love so dearly, and Dr. DeeDee made my dream come true by locating him for me. After 23years, he was opened and receptive to my desire to redevelop a relationship with him. There were no strings attached. I didn't want anything from him but his love and to give him my love. I would never throw in his face anything derogatory about his being missing for the last 20 years,

My heavenly Father had so much compassion for me, despite all the time that I spent in disobedience and rejecting His loving kindness. Oh, how much mercy the Father has bestowed upon me. Now I get the opportunity to bestow that mercy on someone else. Look at me now, a disciple at Spirit of Faith. I am acting like my Daddy and like my pastor. Oh, what a great time to be saved! It is written,

"With long life will He satisfy me and show me how good it is to be one of the saved. Woo, Woo! Now you know my story. **SO WHAT! I AM STILL GOD'S GLAMOROUS GIRL!**

Testimony #14

It all started when I was 7 years old. First, it was just the verbal abuse, and then soon after came the silent punches to my body's fragile frame. I never really knew why my mom rejected me so much as a child. Maybe it was the piercing look of my father that she saw through my eyes or the reality that my existence was a constant reminder of her future being ruined. However, I loved her still. I longed for her approval every day of my life. Of the three children, I was the child that was used as her personal punching bag and personal babysitter. And because there was no father there to protect, I somehow became immune. This led me to believe that this was God's will for my life.

By the time I was 12 and on my way to Jr. High School, I was used to hiding the bruises. I knew how to be nonexistent and how to disappear in a room full of people. None of the school staff seemed to care or even notice that I was being abused and neglected. I was used to being called hateful names and made a fool of. At one point it was so bad that I spent my lunch break eating in the restroom. Degrading and useless is what I thought of myself. Why I was here, was the question I'd ask myself every day.

Then I met the first man that ever loved me; he was 18 years old. We met over the phone during a prank call that went wrong. He actually called my house to play a rude joke, until he heard the sound of my voice, at least that's what I was told. In the beginning our conversations were very simple, nothing too deep. But before I knew it, I was sharing with him my entire heart. I told him everything about the physical and mental abuse. I told him how I wasn't able to have friends, how basically I was mothering my younger sister and brother while my mom caught up on all the things she missed out on because of having me. He was my everything. I held nothing from him. He had become the source of my life. He was the only thing other than my sister and brother that brought me joy. I can still remember the dead silence he gave me as a response to me telling him that my mom was in a relationship with two women and one man, who all live here in the house.

I knew my life wasn't normal, but not until I met him did I ever see myself living another way. Though the abuse was still happening, the pain wasn't the same. I could be beaten with the broom and blood pouring from my face, but be smiling in the inside to know that I'd hear the sound of his voice later. He was my savior, the only one I felt like loved me for me.

It was 9 months later that I decided enough was enough. I had just been kicked in the gut and slapped around numerous times for being caught talking with a neighbor when I should have been cleaning. My face was marked up with bruises there was a gash on my neck, and my body was wrecking with pain. It was time for me to leave. I had to be with my man, I couldn't stand this anymore. I was truly tired. Sure I would miss my siblings, and trust me, I cried so many tears at the thought of never seeing them again. But this time I had to think about me. I never told him I was leaving that day, but so what, he was the one that said I deserved to be treated like a human being instead of cattle.

So instead of school that day, I doubled back and packed my book bag with as many clothes that could fit. I went into my mom's bedroom safe and took about $600.00 and headed out. Looking back at the house, I shed one last tear thinking of what my sister and brother would think when I didn't pick them up from school today. But it wasn't long before the memories of agony flashed before my eyes, and I knew it was time to go, so I went.

I found the first pay phone on Georgia Avenue to make the call to my friend, to let him know where he could pick me up. I still got butterflies at the sound of his voice. When he picked me up, I told him everything: how I was ready to be with him forever now, where I was, and how happy I was to finally be free. He was totally silent. The only words he spoke were, "I'll have my sister pick you up in an hour, so stay put." This was not the response I was expecting, but ok, whatever.

When his sister came to get me, it was nothing like I imagined. As soon as I got into the car, I felt fear. At first I thought it was because we'd never met, but it was definitely something else going on here. She introduced herself, gave me a warm hug, told me to chill out, and enjoy the ride. She said that her brother spoke of me a lot, and she was very familiar with my story, so there was no need to be shy. Funny thing is he never really spoke of her to me. We spent most of the day doing errands and having small talk. Until I couldn't take it anymore and asked, "when I would be seeing my man?" After all, that is what all of this was about for me anyway. With guilt and surprise in her eyes she looked at me and said, "Look, sorry to break it to you like this but, I'm him,."

I could have hurled all over her car when the words actually registered in my mind. I was honestly speechless. Tears began to flow from this girl's eye as she explained that she never really intended for me to leave home. She told me how her mom didn't know that she was into women, how she had been raped on several occasions and found comfort in being with other women. This was truly a mess. I couldn't grasp the concept for the first couple of hours, so I said nothing more than yes or no. but when I came to myself, I had to let this girl know that I wasn't gay. I was in love with what I thought was a man.

Although I wasn't gay, neither could I return home to

the abuse. So we had some serious talking to do. Maybe it was desperation on my part, or even the fact that this person knew me inside and out, but whatever it was, I began to feel comfortable with her. Like no matter what, we would get through this, together. The first thing on the list was to break the news to her mother. That was a disaster. She didn't take it well at all. She immediately told both of us to leave her house, if we intended on carrying this relationship on. So we left.

On a bus to Atlanta Georgia with $250, we would build a life there, we thought. The excitement of it all kept us going for about 3 weeks, but then reality settled in. She found a job at the local grocery store as a meat cutter, while I was still a minor and could rarely been seen in public during the day. We lived in the Peachtree Motel, the most rodent infested motel in the city. Daily I would see prostitutes and heroin addicts rent the rooms out by the hour. The pressure became too much, so we decided to head back to DC. At least we both had family in the area. Besides, her checks were barely enough to cover the daily rate at the motel, and eating became a luxury. Besides the food she lifted from her job, we were drinking the faucet water to stay full.

When we arrived back in DC, we didn't have a secure plan, but it was home. Before we could leave the bus station, she ran into an old high school friend. She told him all about our situation, excluding that fact that we were a couple, and he agreed to allow us to stay in his place until we both found jobs. It was a quiet little room in Maryland that he rented. He was such a gentleman, allowing us to occupy his bed while he took the couch. We both searched for jobs day in and day out. I was still too young and most places wanted a work permit from the state. My friend, landed a position at Burger King.

As time went on Mr. Friend decided to raise the stakes for allowing us to live there, so he pulled my friend aside and gave the ultimatum. Either he could have sex with me or we had to leave on the spot. She came to me and told me the arrangement and I said no. I was afraid; I had never been with a man I barely knew. She was furious with me; she told me that was being childish and stupid. She reminded me how she had made all these sacrifices for me and couldn't do this one thing for us. I thought long and hard. I would have done it but my body wouldn't allow me too. I grew stiff, and we got kicked out.

In tears she went to the pay phone and made a few call. The first was to her play sister in South East and the other to her mom. The next thing you know we were on our way to South East. When we got there, I was terrified. The apartment was identical to the motel we'd just left, but her sister was very warm and open. She had 4 children and a lot of male friends in and out of her house. We stayed there about a week, and then she told me she was going back home, and I had to figure it out from here. This was the beginning of my heartache.

Even though her sister was very pleasant, things automatically changed the second my friend walked out the door. Here was the first place I took my hit of marijuana. They did all sorts of drugs here, everything from crack cocaine to PCP. There were constant knocks at the door from people needing a place to dope up. She was open to it, as long as they supplied her with her drug of choice. I began smoking joints quite frequently, I was too afraid to try the hard stuff. The weed made me feel nice and numb and it kept everything funny. I felt like the weed understood me; it was my friend, the thing I could run to with no explanations. It gave me exactly what I needed, an escape from my pitiful life.

By the time I was 14, I had lived in many drug infested houses. I had been everything from the babysitter to the housekeeper, and life was hard for me. I would meet people one day and pray that they would invite me over just to get a hot meal. Some days I would stand in the subway stations and pretend to be pregnant with a bucket in my hand. Then I met a woman better known as brick house. She was 23 year old mother who took in runaways and taught them how to make a living for themselves. I guess you should call her a disturbed mentor.

The first time she invited me over to her place I was clueless. There were 5 other young ladies there, all between the ages of 13 – 15 years old. She introduced me as fresh meat and told the girls to embrace me as one of their own, and they did. Later that night we all got dolled up to go to a house party I was told. The woman had so many costumes and clothes until we just picked from her pile. She did our makeup and all. For the first time in a long time, I felt so pretty.

We arrived at a beautiful mansion in Ft. Washington, as we walked in she turned to me and whispered, "Don't be afraid, don't be shy, just follow my lead," and I agreed. Once inside the house I found out that these girls were strippers. At first I was a little leery, but then I rationalized with myself and said, "It is just dancing, aint no harm in that." We hit the floor, and the party was on. There were men everywhere, admiring my body, touching and groping. I was very uncomfortable until I saw the money they were placing in my panties. It was more money than I had seen in the past 2 years since I'd been in these streets. I was sold.

That first night I left that party with close to $1,400.00 and I was ready for the next gig. The woman became my teacher. I was watching her every move. She seduced men and women. I watched the way she spoke with confidence, and most of all I watched ho her money was right. We danced in club after club, at firehouses, even for the cops every now and then. The money was flowing, but I was still too young to really establish anything on my own. I always had to depend on Miss Woman. And though I would crash at her place every now and then, I found myself with a pocket full of cash sleeping at the bus station, or trying to party all night and catch a nap at the bus stops in the middle of the night.

Things seemed to be looking up for me until we hosted a weekend party in North Carolina. The party was for some college graduates, all expenses paid, and tips were on us. The first two nights were fun and the money was endless. The guys were very pleasant, not too demanding at all, nothing like the men in the Metropolitan area. They actually seemed to be interested in the dancing, whereas I had gotten used to the groping and slick feels in between your legs at the parties we were used to working.

It wasn't until the third and final party that Miss Woman announced the services we provided would change. Honestly, I was lost. I had no idea what that meant, until I saw lines forming at all of the bedroom doors. By then it wasn't rocket science; these girls were going to turn tricks. And tonight would be the first time in my life that I would have to follow the crowd.

When I entered the room of the man I was supposed to service, I was shaking so badly until I could literally feel my heart pounding, but there was no turning back now. I tried my best to seem as natural as the other girls, but he could tell that I was no pro at this. I lay there as stiff as a board waiting for him to give me instructions. After about 20 minutes of fondling he turned to me and asked me if I was uncomfortable. I hold him no cause I needed this 200 bucks. So he jumped on me and proceeded to finish his business, until he realized I was shaking so badly. He immediately jumped up in total disgust and began to get dressed. I knew that I wouldn't be good at this, and I tried to apologize, but he just threw the money at me and opened the door.

That's when I knew that turning tricks was not for me. As a matter of fact, that's when I realized that hanging with Miss Woman was not for me either. I already had a major problem knowing that she was making major money off of these runaway minors, but to know that she was turning these helpless girls into prostitutes was something I couldn't live with. And as soon as we hit the DMV, I was on my own. I learned enough to start my own hustle and that's exactly what I intended to do.

Oh how thrilled I was to see the Nation's Capital as we sped around 395 to get to Benning Rd. We had a bachelor's party to be at in 45 minutes, so Miss Woman began to lay down the rules while we were still in the van. She began by thanking all of us for a great job done in NC and began to explain that tonight's party was for a police officer who was getting married the next day. The party was to be only 2 hours, and they were going to be big spenders. So after hearing everything being said, I figured I'd at least make this money before I rolled out. Besides I really didn't have another choice. It wasn't as if they even knew I was pulling out.

The party was crazy off the hook. These men of the badge were much worse than your average Joe. I think we danced for maybe 45 minutes, and they were ready to break off into the rooms. That night my job was to stay in the rooms and watch the couples as they interact, and the case that someone was in pain or wanted to stop I was the alarm. As I sat there and watched these young girls sell their bodies for 40 bucks a pop, I was so disgusted.

At that moment I knew I had to find another way to live; this was not me. Some girls were willing and able, while other girls were literally in tears. I felt so bad for these young girls. Here they were selling their bodies to married men for little or no money. Mind you, they each had to pay me 10 bucks per client for being their personal bouncer. So they ended up leaving out of there with 25 bucks maybe. It just wasn't worth it. So I decided that night that I was going back to Georgia. But this time I would say with family. When I got off of the greyhound and smelled downtown Atlanta, I felt like this time would be different. I loved Atlanta, and I was looking forward to building a future here this time. Even though I still talked to the girl it wasn't like that anymore. We grew apart, and I was finally on my own.

I would stay with a cousin there, who would help me get back into school and even look for a little work gig. I was 15 now, so I was due for a work permit according to state laws. Going back to school was an adjustment, but I loved every minute of it. And though I had been tarnished, I felt like a kid again, I actually had a chance at having a real life.

Four week into school and my cousin had company over for the weekend. A really cool high school friend of hers came in from out of town and bought two other random guys along. They partied all weekend together and seemed to have a blast. It wasn't until the last day, that my cousin and her friend went out alone for a few hours and left me to keep the children. While the other guys hung out in the family area, I decided to call it a night.

Before I knew it, I was being raped by both guys right in the presence of my 2 and 7 year old cousins. I was humiliated. Here I was kicking and screaming as these guys I didn't even know took turns raping me. In a state of shock I was able to clean up the bleeding and get myself together by time my cousin returned home. I was so terrified that I didn't mention anything until they all left.

When I did tell her what happened, she just laughed and said maybe I asked for it. I knew at that moment, that no matter how much people say they love and care for you, you're really on your own. So I dropped out of school again and headed back to DC. If I was going to deal with the same lifestyle in Atlanta, then why not be on my own turf and deal with the crap. My life was never the same after that.

After the rape, I became calloused. I did not trust anyone, and I lived quite recklessly. I was always looking for ways to get high, hoping that the weed would make my life seem like a dream. I got back into stripping at the local clubs, and slept on the streets during the day. I had money in my pocket but no desire to live. I wasn't dealing with women in the same fashion, though the entire time my lesbian girlfriend I mentioned earlier, and I remained friends. And I wasn't dealing with men because I was still paralyzed from my previous experience. I was a cold blooded corpse, until the night I met the man of my dreams. I was 16 now and he was 27. We met at a house part where I was dancing. The blunts and alcohol led u straight to the Motel 6. And for whatever reason, I wasn't afraid of him. He never intimidated me, and so I went all the way with him. This was my first consensual experience with a man, and I was the initiator. He made it very clear that this was a one night thing only, but I didn't care either way. I had no emotions; this was just fun. So much fun that he left me with a baby on the way.

As soon as it was confirmed that I was with child, the emotions that were bottled up for so many years all came to the light. I think I cried the first two weeks, some were tears of joy, confusion, anger, and pain. What was I going to do? Abortion wasn't an option, I was sleeping on the streets, barely eating, how was I going to have a healthy baby. Without any other options, I called my lesbian friend.

Though I knew that homosexuality was definitely not my cup of tea, I moved in with my lesbian friend because I knew I would be safe. I knew she wouldn't leave me high and dry, like so many of the others. She was established-now, so no rules or regulations. Her only request was that I allow her to love my baby as her own. How could I disagree, free room and board with someone I was already used to.

I barely even knew I was pregnant, no morning sickness or weight gain. You couldn't even tell I was pregnant until the 8th month. All of a sudden it looked like I swallowed a basketball. My mind wad different now that I knew I had a baby on the way; I started to actually think about what I wanted out of life. And the one think I knew I wanted was for my daughter to have a father. Any by no means was I going to raise this child in a lesbian relationship. I had no idea how I would break the news to my lesbian friend. She had prepared the entire apartment for the baby's arrival.

Even her mom had come around once she found out I was having a little girl. All the animosity she had towards me in the earlier years seemed to dissipate. She almost became a second mom to me. Everything about women and pregnancy I asked her. She taught me a lot; said she didn't want me to end up being a sorry excuse for a mother to this innocent child.

When I gave birth to my daughter, she had everything a child could want except a father. She was not to worry because I was going to fix that. Living with my lesbian friend lasted about 6 months. When I heard her telling my daughter to call her dada, I knew it was time for me to go. I just didn't know where I was going. Things between me and my lesbian friend got worse. We were fighting every day. The only common ground we had was the baby. And that wasn't really common, because I hated my daughter being around such confusion.

The last fight we had was the worse. The police were called in and my daughter and I were put out. Everything was in my lesbian friend's name and she made sure she told the cops that. She insisted the baby stay in her care, because she knew I had not place to go. However, the law said that the mother keeps her child until proven in the courts that she is unfit.

For the first few days we stayed in the local laundry room. My daughter had severe asthma, so I needed to be close to an electrical outlet for her machine. She was a happy baby, never fussy and always smiling. Often times during the day, we'd walk and walk, and I'd tell her all kinds of stories of how good our life would be one day. I loved her, and I knew in my heart that this wouldn't last always.

I knew that sleeping in the laundry mat wasn't healthy for any infant, so I bit the bullet and contacted my mother. It had been almost 4 years since I had spoken to my mother. She never looked for me, and I was too afraid to contact her, even thought there were so many times I wanted to. But this time I had no other choice, this was about my daughter being safe.

When I heard her voice I began to cry. Even through all the drama and abuse, I loved my mother, I longed for her acceptance. I kept it simple, I told her I was living in the street with my 6 month old baby, and I needed a place to live. She asked me if I was receiving any kind of welfare assistance, and I told her yes. The agreement was I could rent a room in her home, for the total amount of my welfare check. This was $239.00. I took the offer, hopped on the bus and headed back uptown.

We arrived at the house with a book bag of clothing, and the baby's asthma machine. We were greeted with the total look of disappointment and I knew it would be hard living here. My mom made it clear that this was a business agreement and nothing more. The one part she left out over the phone was that in order for me to live there, I had to attend church services every Sunday and Wednesday. I never knew my mother to be religious, but her house, her rules, and I wasn't going to put up a fight.

It felt good to be back in my old neighborhood. I ran into a lot of old associates, and things were much different now that I was all grown up with a baby. I often thought to myself, this could be a new beginning for me and my mom.

When I first stepped foot into my mom's church, I felt like things in my life were going to change. I was never a church going person so this was all very new to me. I'll never forget the first sermon I had ever heard. The preacher's sermon was about burning in hell for the sins of your youth. I was so scared I asked for a conference immediately afterwards.

The pastor kindly met with me that day, for about 4 hours we talked. He explained every reason why hell was real and if I continued to live the way I was living, I would have a first class ticket. That was all it took for me. I joined that day.

Six months later I was getting married to the first guy in my neighborhood that paid me any attentions. I didn't want to burn in hell for fornication, so the pastor told me to marry or burn. Needless to say, I married just at 18. Between church services and rehearsals, I began to be in church at least six days a week.

In the beginning it was great. It felt like God was pleased. But I still hadn't done what I needed to do to help me and my daughter. I had not diploma, no job, and no vision for my future. Every time I would speak of this the church leaders they'd politely tell me my focus should be on being a housewife. So I was obedient in hopes that I would be in good with God.

Before my husband and I could even figure each other out, I was pregnant. Not long after I was on baby number four. Every time I gave birth, I was pregnant again. After two miscarriages and five children something had to give. My soul began to become restless and worn out. Every month's calendar was filled with revivals, building fund services, youth activities, and so much more. I just couldn't keep up.

So as usual I would set up a conference time to speak with my pastor about this overwhelming shift that was taking place in my life. In the initial meeting I share with him how unhappy and unfilled I was in my marriage. How I was never in love to begin with and everything in my life

I was doing out of obligation instead of genuine love. I felt like a failure, a hypocrite.

There I was living in a two bedroom apartment with five children. Still collecting benefits from the government. Attached to a man who had no ambition or vision for his life. Was all I good for was getting pregnant. I told him my entire heart, and he seemed really honestly concerned. Shortly after our session, he put me to work in the ministry. He said I wasn't busy enough, so the devil was playing on my time being idle.

I held every position from usher, Jr. church leader, kitchen cook, fundraising coordinator, step team coach, praise dance leader, youth minister of evangelism, and , and any other office that was vacant. I was so engrossed with ministry that my family no long was priority. I didn't know how to balance working for the Lord, being a wife and raising five children. I felt like I had to choose, so I chose God.

Ultimately after becoming very familiar with the structure of the ministry, the pastor felt that I was an asset to the growth of the ministry and began to have me work closer to him in the area of church administrator/secretary. Often times I was required to stay late hours, and as soon as he knew that I was loyal to the ministry, he made his move.

When we first began to have this sexual relationship, I was plagued with guilt. I felt filthy like a whore. But he explained it away every time, said that he was weak and I was the only one he could confide in. so I kept his secret and mine too. The affair lasted for 3 long years.

It was Passion Week service in 2008 when a minister stood up to give an announcement. The announcement was that the pastor had touched her teenage daughter in an inappropriate manner. Not only had he touched her daughter, he was in a 15 year relationship with her also. Soon after, many women came forward to say that they had been involved with him in the same manner. I was completely confused and felt like an idiot. That evening when I left the service, I knew God told me never to look back, and I didn't. Now there I was displaced after 12 years of devotion to this church. I had no idea what to do or where to turn. This was my only encounter with God, it was my source of religion, I thought.

For years I had been driving pass Spirit of Faith and was always interested in visiting. So this Sunday I decided to pull in and check it out. The first time I heard Pastor Mike speak, I knew this was the man of God that would lead me to my next level. I immediately set up a conference with Dr. DeeDee to receive instruction for my healing process. With a gently spirit, love, and compassion she looked me square in the eyes and told me, that even after all I'd shared with her, I was still a woman of God.

It's been a little over a year since I joined this awesome ministry. And I can honestly say that my life has changed in the best way. I see and understand God more than I ever have in all my life. There are no cords of condemnation that bind me to my past any longer, and my mind is being renewed every day. In the times that I feel week I look to the word of God now instead of my emotions and failures.

When I look in the mirror now, I really do believe that I am still a woman of God. No you know my story; **"So What," I am still God's Glamorous Girl.**